1. IX. 06

PUEBLO INDIAN TEXTILES

STUDIES IN AMERICAN INDIAN ART

The publication of this book was made possible by generous support from the National Endowment for the Arts and the Weatherhead Foundation.

PUEBLO INDIAN

with a Catalogue of the School of American Research Collection

TEXTILES:
A Living Tradition

Awatsireh

KATE PECK KENT

SCHOOL OF AMERICAN RESEARCH PRESS : SANTA FE, NEW MEXICO

SCHOOL OF AMERICAN RESEARCH PRESS
Post Office Box 2188
Santa Fe, New Mexico 85701

DISTRIBUTED BY UNIVERSITY OF WASHINGTON PRESS

EDITOR: Jane Kepp
PHOTOGRAPHER: Deborah Flynn
ILLUSTRATOR: Arminta Neal
DESIGNER: Linnea Gentry
COMPOSITOR: Business Graphics
PRINTER: Thomson-Shore, Inc.

Library of Congress Cataloging in Publication Data

Kent, Kate Peck.
  Pueblo Indian textiles.
  (Studies in American Indian art)
  "With a catalogue of the School of American Research collection."
  Bibliography: p.
  Includes index.
  1. Pueblo Indians—Textile industry and fabrics. 2. Indians of North America—Southwest,
New—Textile industry and fabrics. 3. Pueblo Indians—Textile industry and
fabrics—Catalogs. 4. Indians of North America—Southwest, New—Textile industry and
fabrics—Catalogs. 5. School of American Research (Santa Fe, N.M.)—Catalogs. I. School of
American Research (Santa Fe, N.M.) II. Title. III. Series.
E99.P9K46   1983   746.1'4'08997   83-3346
ISBN 0-933452-07-1
ISBN 0-933452-08-X (pbk.)

Frontispiece. At a Basket Dance at San Ildefonso Pueblo, the dancers wear traditional Pueblo
costumes. The drummer, standard bearer, and chorus are clad in commercial cloth pants of
Spanish design and shirts that probably reflect early Anglo-American influence. Some wear
black breechcloths and traditional Pueblo headbands. Painting by Awa Tsireh (Alfonso
Roybal) of San Ildefonso Pueblo, about 1923. (SAR P.1.)

Contents

List of Illustrations

Frontispiece. Painting by Awa Tsireh of a Basket Dance at San Ildefonso Pueblo, about 1923.

Plates

Foreword

For the Pueblo Indians of the American Southwest, weaving and decorating textiles is a tradition that reaches almost two thousand years into the past, yet this dynamic art form continues today as a vital part of Pueblo ceremonialism. The Pueblos' earliest direct ancestors produced rabbit-fur blankets and simple fabrics from wild plant fibers using basic finger techniques. At about A.D. 600, they added cotton fiber acquired from tribes to the south. Then, in the years approaching A.D. 1000, a revolutionary change occurred when the loom became widely used and domesticated cotton began to be grown locally. With this new technology and with finer fabrics, a creative explosion took place in the fashioning of breechcloths, kilts, shawls, dresses, shirts, belts, sashes, and a variety of other items that became essential elements of the prehistoric Pueblo textile tradition.

Beginning in the late 1500s, Spanish settlers, priests, and military men dominated the Southwest, to be replaced first by Mexican and later, in 1848, by American rule. The Spaniards, by introducing wool, commercial cloth, indigo dye, and some new techniques, created major changes in the Pueblo fabric tradition. With the Americans came the railroads, which brought commercial goods in quantity, and the mission schools, which imposed Anglo standards of dress on the Indians. As a result, traditional Pueblo weaving was nearly eradicated.

Today, the Hopis of Arizona continue to weave some ceremonial clothing in the old ways, while the New Mexico Pueblos tend to make traditional forms of costume from commercial fabric and to decorate them with embroidery in designs of prehistoric ancestry. At Pueblo ceremonials, the enduring strength of this craft is as obvious as are the changes it has undergone. Elegant costumes of handwoven cloth mix with items of modern manufacture to form an integral part of the ritual drama. The traditional Pueblo styles, regardless of the materials from which they are manufactured, stand out as symbols of continuity with the Pueblos' ancient past.

This volume documents the history of Pueblo textiles, introduces the tools, techniques, and raw materials used to create Pueblo fabrics, and skillfully describes the products of this magnificent craft. The quality of this book is a tribute to Kate Kent, who brings to her work a sensitivity and authority that grow from a lifetime of studying traditional fabrics of the Southwest. During a year as research curator at the School of American Research Indian Art Center, and subsequently with support by the School through a grant from the National Endowment for the Arts, Kent wrote the text for this book and chose from the School's collections the best items to illustrate the nature of Pueblo textiles. She also has catalogued the entire collection of Pueblo textiles in the School's Indian Art Center; a full listing appears in the Appendix.

The writing and publication of this volume were made possible by grants from the National Endowment for the Arts and the Weatherhead Foundation. We at the School of American Research are deeply grateful for the support of both organizations and for their interest in American Indian art that has allowed us to present this detailed documentation of traditional Pueblo Indian textiles.

DOUGLAS W. SCHWARTZ
School of American Research

Acknowledgments

Many people facilitated the research for this book and assisted in its preparation. I wish to thank collectively the staff members of the following museums for aiding my studies of their collections: American Museum of Natural History; Arizona State Museum; Denver Art Museum; Denver Museum of Natural History; Laboratory of Anthropology, Museum of New Mexico; Maxwell Museum of Anthropology; Milwaukee Public Museum; Museum of Northern Arizona; National Museum of Natural History, Smithsonian Institution; and Peabody Museum, Harvard University. Barbara Stanislawski deserves special thanks for making available the collections and records of the School of American Research and for furnishing work space and office support.

All of us engaged in the study of southwestern textiles are indebted to Joe Ben Wheat for sharing his vast knowledge of the subject with us. His findings on yarn characteristics, dyes, and weave technicalities have been particularly useful in dating and identifying classic period textiles in the School's collections.

Answers to the questions asked by Martin Etter, the first editor of the manuscript for this book, have, I believe, added considerable interest to the text. Jane Kepp did the final editing and deserves full credit for correcting inaccuracies, improving the flow of language, and organizing the catalogue material in the Appendix.

In late 1981, Bobbi Culbert undertook the study of European-derived Pueblo textiles at the School of American Research. Her preliminary findings are incorporated in the brief section of the text dealing with that part of the School's collection.

Except where noted otherwise, the excellent line drawings in this book are the work of Arminta Neal, and the photographs, of Deborah Flynn. Barbara Cavallo, Ellen Diethelm, and Willa Walker assisted with the typing of the manuscript and catalogue data.

Finally, let me thank the National Endowment for the Arts and the Weatherhead Foundation for the financial support that allowed me to carry on the research and writing of the book, and Dr. Douglas W. Schwartz, president of the School of American Research, for his continued encouragement throughout.

It seems appropriate to dedicate this volume to the memory of the late Frederic H. Douglas, who undertook the first serious study of Pueblo textiles, and to Alfred F. Whiting, whose unpublished papers furnished valuable data on several classes of Hopi textiles.

KATE PECK KENT

PUEBLO INDIAN TEXTILES

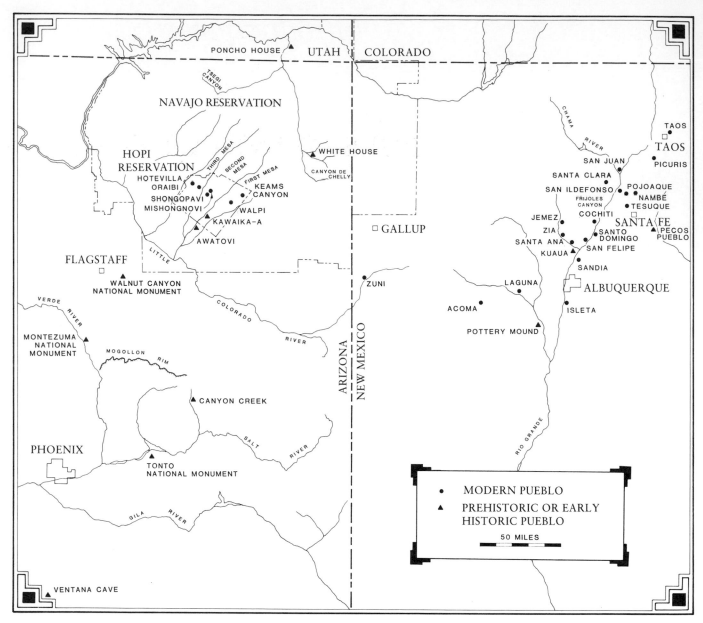

Figure 1. Locations of contemporary Pueblo villages and archaeological sites mentioned in the text. (Map by Carol Cooperrider.)

Introduction

The sixteenth-century Spaniards, entering the region we know today as the American Southwest, found the natives of the land living in compact villages, or pueblos, of stone-walled or mud-walled houses. These Indians practiced intensive agriculture, had a complex socioreligious system, and were skilled in many crafts, especially pottery making, basketry, and weaving. Spanish reports suggest that there were at least seventy villages in the mid-1500s (Schroeder 1979:236–54). The contemporary Pueblo Indians, descendants of these earlier people, live in thirty-one villages: nineteen in New Mexico and twelve in the Hopi country of northeastern Arizona (Fig.1).

The Spaniards noted especially that the Indians they encountered from the vicinity of present-day El Paso northward were well clothed in cotton textiles, in marked contrast to the generally naked peoples they had previously met in their march north from the Valley of Mexico. Spanish accounts express astonishment at the beauty and quantity of the fabrics worn by the people and offered as gifts. They mention embroidered and painted shirts, mantas or shawls, sashes, and kilts or breechcloths, though they give little precise information about technical processes or design styles. Luxan, on the occasion of Antonio de Espejo's visit to Awatovi in 1583, recorded: "Hardly had we pitched camp when about one thousand Indians came laden with maize, ears of green corn, pinole, tamales, and firewood, and they offered it all, together with six hundred widths of blankets small and large, white and painted, so that it was a pleasant sight to behold" (Hammond and Rey 1929:98).

We know that the kinds of textiles seen by the Spaniards had been made and used by southwestern people for hundreds of years (Kent 1957, 1983).

Our evidence consists of some 3,000 textile fragments and a few complete fabrics from archaeological sites dating mostly between A.D. 1000 and 1400 (Fig. 2), and of costumes depicted in the fifteenth-century Pueblo murals of Kuaua (Fig. 3), Awatovi, Kawaika-a, and Pottery Mound (Dutton 1963, Hibben 1975, Smith 1952). The oldest examples of Anasazi, or prehistoric Pueblo, textiles, dated between A.D. 200 and 600, were made by finger techniques from wild plant and animal fibers. Cotton, which was introduced into southern Arizona between A.D. 100 and 600, appears in a few of these Anasazi textiles shortly before 700. Loom-woven cotton fabrics have been found in a few northern sites dated between 700 and 1000, but the first clear evidence for the cultivation of cotton north of the Mogollon Rim dates after A.D. 1000.

In addition to using native-grown cotton, early Pueblo weavers worked with apocynum (Indian hemp), yucca leaf fiber, fur, and feather cord. Tools found in many of the prehistoric sites indicate that cotton was spun with the same type of stick-and-whorl spindle still in use today (see Fig. 15). The re-

Figure 2. Negative patterning in black and white decorates a painted cotton blanket from Hidden House (about A.D. 1250) in central Arizona. Similar blankets were probably presented to the Spaniards three hundred years later. Width 64".
(Courtesy Arizona State Museum, The University of Arizona, photo by E. B. Sayles.)

sulting yarn was fashioned by finger processes into socks, bags, nets, and braids or was woven into cloth on a wide upright loom or a backstrap loom. Weaving on the loom was a man's art and continued to be so until recently. Anasazi weavers knew a limited range of natural dyes, including brick red, brown, black, yellow, and pale blue.

Prehistoric textiles show more complex designs and varied techniques than do historic pieces. They were elaborately patterned in dynamic designs by tie-and-dye, weft-wrap openwork, gauze weave (Fig. 4), interlocking twill tapestry, irregular twill weaves, brocade, and weft-float, techniques that are no longer employed by Pueblo craftsmen.

At the time of their arrival, the Spaniards found cotton growing at pueblos in the Rio Grande Valley as far north as the mouth of the Chama River, at Acoma, and at Hopi to the west (Jones 1936). Spanish accounts are unclear about whether the plant was grown at Zuni, although Fray Marcos de Niza in 1539 spoke of Zuni houses that were full of cotton cloth (Riley 1975:139). Judging from the historical accounts, it is probably safe to assume that some of this cloth was woven at Zuni but most was obtained from the Hopi villages, where cotton was grown in great quantities to supply a thriving industry that produced textiles both for domestic use and for export. Luxan, for example, described in 1583 a march of "two leagues, one of them through cotton fields" between the first and second Hopi mesas (Hammond and Rey 1929:101).

During the sixteenth century, the Zuni towns sat at the crossroads of major trade routes running to the south and southwest, northwest toward the Hopi country, and north and east to the Rio Grande Valley, Pecos Pueblo, and the southern Great Plains. Cotton cloth was surely important among the goods carried along these routes. Trade goods passing through Zuni and other pueblos included turquoise from New Mexico, shell and coral from the Gulf of California and the Pacific, parrot and macaw feathers from Mexico, worked hides from the Great Plains, salt and semiprecious stones from various localities, and blankets from Hopi. Indians encountered by de Soto in eastern Arkansas or Texas had cotton blankets obtained, they said, from people to the west (Bohrer, in press), and a cotton blanket thought to be of Pueblo manufacture was found with a burial near Bakersfield, California (Gifford and Schenk 1926:104–105, Pl. 2). The sixteenth-century sources attest that parties of men accompanied by interpreters undertook lengthy trips to other trade centers: Coronado was visited at Zuni by such a party from Pecos Pueblo, and Ca-

Figure 3. In a kiva mural at Kuaua Pueblo (Coronado State Monument, N.M.), a male figure wears a black kilt with a white sash. (Courtesy Museum of New Mexico, photo no. 80335.)

beza de Vaca and Fray Marcos both met Pueblo traders as far south as northern Mexico (Riley 1975:138–40).

The pattern of trade described for the sixteenth-century Pueblos had, of course, been established long before the arrival of Europeans in the Southwest. Although the role of textiles in this trade is difficult to document because of their poor preservation in archaeological sites, there is little doubt of their importance.

The indigenous clothing of the Pueblos included such items as breech-cloths, kilts, mantas, blanket-dresses (Fig. 5), openwork shirts and leggings, woven belts, and braided sashes. While many of these articles served as daily wear in pre-Spanish and early historic times, they survive today mainly in ritual use, although they are not in themselves sacred. A few, such as the black blanket-dress and the long red belt, may be worn on secular occasions when a person wishes to establish through costume his or her ethnic identity. Relatively few innovations have been made in handwoven forms: chief among these are the Spanish-style wool blanket, or serape, and the heavier, blanket-like rugs woven since the late 1800s. Thus, although many prehistoric weaving techniques have fallen into disuse, and handspun yarn and natural dyes have largely been replaced by commercial yarns and bright synthetic dyes, the forms and functions of Pueblo textiles have remained remarkably unchanged since prehistoric times.

This book is devoted to textiles made in the indigenous tradition during the classic period of historic Pueblo weaving, 1848 to 1880, and to those that represent more recent modifications of classic forms. Less attention is paid to a second Pueblo textile tradition of comparatively recent origin, derived from a Euro-American base. It includes articles such as silk shawls and Pendleton blankets, as well as certain forms of clothing made from commercial cloth that show strong Spanish or Anglo-American stylistic influence. Some of these textiles are worn by dancers and some by Pueblo men and women dressed for formal occasions. A history of the adaptation of commercial textiles to Pueblo needs and tastes remains to be written; it would actually be a study of acculturation in costume, not of textiles per se. A few typical examples are illustrated for the record, but they are not interpreted in technical or historical terms.

The literature on traditional Pueblo textiles is limited. While there are dozens of publications about Navajo weaving—books, pamphlets, articles, and catalogues—the indigenous tradition from which the Navajos learned their

Figure 4. A child's gauze-weave cotton poncho from Ventana Cave (A.D. 1100–1400) in southern Arizona is decorated with a motif in weft-wrap openwork on the chest. Length 28". (Courtesy Arizona State Museum, The University of Arizona, photo by Helga Teiwes.)

art remains poorly documented and relatively unknown to the general public. It has received serious attention from only a handful of scholars.

The *Indian Leaflet Series* of the Denver Art Museum, written by the late Frederic H. Douglas between 1930 and 1940, remains a basic source of information about the textiles of the Rio Grande Pueblos, Acoma, Laguna, and Zuni. Leslie Spier's 1924 paper adds substantially to the information on weaving at Zuni at the turn of the century. There is a bit more information in print for the Hopis (see Colton 1938 and 1965, Douglas 1938, Hough 1918, Kent 1940, Stephen 1936, Whiting 1977, and Wright 1979), but our knowledge of the history and use of some textiles remains incomplete. I have been aided substantially by Dr. Douglas's unpublished field notes (1935–1938) on weaving in the New Mexico pueblos and by several unpublished papers on Hopi textiles by the late Alfred F. Whiting. Conversations with contemporary Pueblo craftsmen have helped me understand certain technical processes and also the economic and social importance of contemporary textiles. The general reader will find a convenient summary of the available information on classic and contemporary Pueblo textiles in the Museum of New Mexico guidebook by Nancy Fox (1978). Virginia Roediger's 1941 book contains illustrations that are a helpful guide to Pueblo ceremonial costumes.

There is a good reason for the general lack of public knowledge about, and interest in, Pueblo textiles. Quite simply, they were woven not for tourist sale but to meet the needs of an internal market. Except for a few forms such

Figure 5. Two Hopi girls wear traditional, handwoven, black wool blanket-dresses with commercial cloth mantas, about 1902. (Courtesy Southwest Museum, Los Angeles, Calif., photo by A. C. Vroman.)

as belts, sashes, and certain contemporary embroideries, they have not proved usable by Anglo buyers. The modest number of blankets and rugs woven for external markets has never commanded the attention that has been given to Navajo textiles (Kent 1976).

Much of the fascination of Navajo weaving lies in its variety and innovativeness of design and in the ways in which it has changed through the years to meet the demands of the market place. Traditional Pueblo textiles do not have this kind of appeal. They must be appreciated, instead, for their historical significance, their cultural authenticity, and the technical proficiency that many of them display. Pueblo textiles have in the past been included alongside Navajo blankets and rugs in general catalogues of southwestern textiles, where they are largely overwhelmed by the number, variety, and visual flamboyance of the Navajo pieces. It is hoped that the present book will furnish a better perspective on the importance of traditional Pueblo textiles.

The Evolution of Pueblo Textiles in Historic Times

I

The history of Pueblo textiles since the arrival of the Spaniards in 1540 is best considered in four time periods: the period of Spanish domination, 1540–1848; the "classic" period of historic Pueblo weaving, 1848–1880; the period of growing Anglo-American influence and the decline of weaving, 1880–1920; and the revival of certain forms of Pueblo textiles that led to the contemporary picture, 1920–1950.

SPANISH INFLUENCE, 1540 TO 1848

The Spanish presence in the Southwest changed Pueblo textiles in many ways but did not destroy the art of weaving. In fact, during the first century of Spanish domination, the production of utilitarian textiles probably increased because the settlers, cut off from New Spain and unable or unwilling to weave sufficient goods to meet their own needs, exploited Pueblo weavers.

The original contingent of four hundred colonists under Don Juan de Oñate settled at the pueblo of San Juan in 1598. While these settlers under-

Figure 6. This shirt of white, commercial cotton cloth was made and embroidered in red and black wool at Jemez Pueblo in about 1950. The stepped elements on the body of the shirt and on the sleeves are actually half of the standard cloud motif commonly embroidered on kilt ends. Body 27" long, 30" wide. (SAR T.628.)

stood the technology of the European treadle loom, there is no evidence that they brought loom parts with them or constructed machines during the first three decades after their arrival. The settlers brought churro sheep, whose wool is eminently suited for spinning and weaving, but these they used for meat rather than fiber. The neighboring Pueblos were forced to support the Spaniards with tributes of food and textiles. In 1635, Fray Alonso de Benavides, the Franciscan official in charge of the New Mexico missions, noted: "It has been established by the first governors of New Mexico, and is being continued by order of the viceroy that each house pay a tribute consisting of a cotton blanket, the best of which are about a *vara* and a half square. . ." (Hodge, Hammond, and Rey 1945:169). A vara is a unit of measurement equal to 31–34 inches; Benavides was describing the typical proportions of a traditional Pueblo manta.

In addition to demanding the products of native looms, the Spaniards commandeered Pueblo labor after 1638 to help weave on treadle looms that by then had been constructed in the Santa Fe workshop of Governor Luis de Rosas. The Spaniards also introduced the European technique of knitting with needles early in the seventeenth century, and by mid-century the Pueblos were knitting hundreds of pairs of wool socks for distribution to the colonists. Knitting and crocheting eventually replaced the finger techniques of interlinking and looping by which socks, shirts, bags, and leggings had been made prehistorically.

Enforced labor and demands for tribute contributed to the unrest and dissatisfaction that culminated in the Pueblo Revolt of 1680. They must also have left little time for weaving the elaborately patterned fabrics of prehistoric times, with their intricate weaves and dynamic designs. Embroidery, which demanded less time, became the decorative technique par excellence, particularly among the Rio Grande Pueblos (Fig. 6). Embroidered designs were applied to the warp borders of plain-weave or twill-weave fabrics. Many of the motifs used in prehistoric woven textile designs survive today in these embroidered borders. Embroidered fabrics from Zuni, Acoma, and Jemez sometimes also display the single motif adopted from the Spaniards—a small, stylized flower. The historic emphasis on embroidery, however, may not have arisen solely from the wish to produce decorative fabrics quickly. New dyes, commercial yarn, and metal needles may have contributed to its rise, and embroidered altar cloths and church vestments imported by the Spaniards might have served as models.

Sheep became available to the Pueblos early in the seventeenth century, and by 1650 wool as well as cotton blankets were produced on the traditional upright loom. The Pueblos never discarded this loom in favor of the European treadle loom, nor did they modify their methods of spinning; the stick-and-whorl spindle was used to spin wool yarn exactly as cotton had been spun for centuries. Spanish wool cards for combing fibers straight before spinning were adopted at an unknown date, however, and are still used by the Hopis to prepare both cotton and wool. The European hole-and-slot heddle (Sturtevant 1977) was used by the Pueblos in belt weaving for a time, but it was discarded for the traditional string-loop heddle in the twentieth century (see Figs. 19 and 21).

After 1600, the use of wool and new dyes changed the appearance of Pueblo textiles. Trade invoices record the importation of indigo dye from Mexico in the 1600s and of commercial wool cloth that was raveled for its red yarns.

No complete examples of seventeenth-century serapes, or blankets, have come down to us. Still, like eighteenth- and early nineteenth-century Pueblo blankets, they probably conformed to Spanish taste, being patterned by simple weft stripes (Fig. 7). They were probably longer (as measured along the warps) than wide, a shape introduced by the Spaniards, and weft-faced rather than open in weave like traditional Pueblo plain-weave cotton blankets, in which both warp and weft are of about the same value visually.

Women's clothing does not seem to have changed during the years of Spanish domination. In contrast, at some time before Anglo-American presence was felt in the Southwest, most Pueblo men adopted Spanish-style white cotton pants slit up to the knee on the outer leg seams (Fig. 7). Originally these pants had no gusset at the crotch, which was not sewn shut but was covered with a breechcloth. Men also adopted muslin and velveteen shirts, the traditional woven shirt being largely reserved for ceremonial occasions.

Well before 1700, the Pueblos taught Navajo women how to spin and weave. While Navajo looms were identical to those of their instructors, Nav-

Figure 7. A Hopi weaver in 1901 has a partially completed blanket on the loom. He wears traditional white cotton pants with slit legs. (Courtesy Museum of New Mexico, photo no. 37527, photo by Carl N. Werntz.)

ajo weavers developed certain idiosyncratic tricks that distinguish their work from that of the Pueblos. By the early 1700s, the Navajos were acknowledged masters of weaving, trading their goods to Spaniards and Pueblos alike. Relieved of the pressure to produce mantas and blankets for the Spaniards, Pueblo weavers must have turned their efforts to filling the needs of their own people for traditional items of clothing.

CLASSIC PERIOD TEXTILES, 1848 TO 1880

By the mid-nineteenth century, when the United States wrested control of the Southwest from Mexico, Pueblo textiles showed the effects of some three hundred years of Spanish influence. Even so, the technology of spinning and weaving had not changed, nor had the forms of traditional articles of wearing apparel. The first three decades of American domination, ending with the coming of the railroad in 1880, are called the classic period. Textiles from these years make up the nucleus of our fine old museum collections and define traditional Pueblo weaving for people today.

Men continued to act as weavers and embroiderers, except at Zuni, where both men and women practiced these arts, and at Acoma, where some women did embroidery. The fibers and dyes of Spanish times continued in use, but after 1875 commercial wool yarns, cotton string, and aniline dyes became available and were used with increasing frequency.

Most traditional articles—mantas, kilts, shirts, and breechcloths—were woven in a white (usually cotton) and a dark blue or black (wool) version. There are, for example, six versions of the woman's manta, at least four varieties of breechcloths, and three or four different kinds of shirts, as well as differences in the embroidery motifs used at Hopi, Zuni, and Acoma. This diversity strongly suggests that classic period textiles are a mix of several types, each of which was originally characteristic of a different Pueblo group.

The more elaborate articles—those painted, embroidered, braided, crocheted, or done in "Hopi brocade"—were reserved for feast days. Black wool dresses, red belts, and simple shoulder blankets survived through the period as ordinary wear for women. Underdresses and undergarments were added only after 1875 or 1880 in most New Mexico pueblos. Men continued to wear shoulder blankets, belts, hair ties, garters, knit leggings, and sometimes breechcloths along with their Mexican-style pants and shirts.

Unquestionably weaving was a more important occupation in the nineteenth-century Hopi towns than in the New Mexico pueblos. The Hopis manufactured traditional textiles and traded them to New Mexico villages where little or no weaving was done, continuing the pattern established in late prehistoric times. Palmer (1870:599) states in his government report on the Hopis that "their manufacture of women's robes and blankets is highly prized by all the Pueblo Indians of New Mexico, and these articles are quite an item of trade with them." Stevenson (n.d.:118) reports that in 1879

> the manufacture of cotton embroidered ceremonial blankets, dance kilts and sashes of the same material, white cotton blankets with red and blue borders, worn principally by women, women's black diagonal cloth dresses and wraps of the same, and women's belts was a great industry among the Hopi Indians. The trading of these articles to all the Pueblo tribes from Taos to Isleta dates so far back that there is no knowledge handed down of the time when the Hopi goods were first introduced among the other Pueblos. The Zuni, too, although perhaps their trading was not to be mentioned in comparison with the Hopi, carried the women's dresses, wraps and belts to Taos and the other villages.

Beaglehole (1937:81–86) described traditional Hopi practices of exchange within and between villages. Handwoven cloth figured prominently, serving as a payment for curing and as a gift from the groom's family to the bride at the wedding ceremony or from a grandfather to a new baby in the family. Cloth might also be bartered for other items during visits between villagers at times of ceremonies.

In trading with other tribes, the Hopis preferred to wait at home for visitors to come to them (Beaglehole 1937:81–86). Occasionally a man or a group of men might gather up mantas and other woven goods from several Hopi villages and make an expedition to Zuni, Acoma, or the Rio Grande pueblos. These men went to the house of a "trade friend" where they would be well received and supplied with food for the return journey. They spread their wares out in the plaza, word went around the community, and the exchanges began.

In return for fabrics, the Rio Grande Pueblos supplied the Hopis with commercial red wool blankets to be raveled for weaving or embroidery yarns, blue carbonate, buffalo skins, hoes, shells, and turquoise. One long shell necklace was the equivalent of two mantas, and a buckskin or about three pounds of indigo could be exchanged for one manta.

The Havasupais, Navajos, and White Mountain Apaches also obtained textiles from Hopi. A Havasupai might trade, for example, two large buckskins and a smaller one for a bed-sized blanket, or a shell necklace or a five-pound sack of red ocher for a white wedding blanket "with red stripes" (Beaglehole 1937:85; the reference may possibly be to the woman's white manta with red and indigo blue border stripes.) The Havasupais also supplied piñon nuts and mescal to the Hopis.

Navajo traders received cotton and wool ceremonial costumes in return for meat and hides, and the White Mountain Apaches brought deerskin moccasins, bows and arrows, and mescal to Hopi to barter for colored yarns, belts, and blankets. In the mid-1800s, Mormon settlers exchanged horses for Hopi blankets. Trade, in short, gave impetus to the production of woven goods at Hopi throughout the nineteenth century and, indeed, well into the twentieth century.

ANGLO-AMERICAN INFLUENCE, 1880 TO 1920

The Denver and Rio Grande Railroad and the Atchison, Topeka, and Santa Fe had pushed into New Mexcio by 1880. With their coming, commercial yarns and dyes, yard goods, and sewing machines became readily available to

Figure 8. Changes in Hopi dress in the early twentieth century are exemplified by the calico dresses that show beneath Pendleton blankets worn as mantas. Only the two older women wear the traditional black manta. The boys are dressed in American-style overalls. (Courtesy John P. Wilson, photo by Joseph Mora.)

the Eastern Pueblos, and shawls, Pendleton blankets, and all manner of factory-produced clothing quickly replaced traditional clothing for everyday wear. As one old Tewa man put it in 1938, "people wore new kinds of clothes when the trains came" (Douglas 1935–38).

Perhaps even more important than the railroad in forcing change in everyday costume was the education of Indian children in government and mission schools that were established after 1880. Anglo teachers imposed their ideas of modesty and of appropriate clothing styles on the children. Girls learned to make their own clothes on sewing machines. By the time of the First World War, the younger generation had stopped wearing most traditional clothing except on special occasions. Exceptions were the black dress and red belt, worn until quite recently by adult women over a cotton dress.

Although change came more slowly to the isolated Hopis, government reports for the 1880s list clothing among the items distributed to them annually. In 1887 a government school was opened at Keams Canyon. In exchange for bringing their children to school, fathers were given axes, hammers, and lamps, and mothers were given dress cloth. Native clothes were taken from the children at school, to be replaced by shoes, shirts, underwear, and khaki pants or overalls for the boys and by dresses, petticoats, shoes, and aprons for the girls (Udall 1969:92; Simmons 1942:89, 90, 94; Neville 1952:45). Children returning home from school retained their American-style clothes.

By 1910, seven traders had set up shop on the Hopi reservation, stocking staple food items, hardware, and cloth. It was not long before the Hopis began to get cloth at the trading post in exchange for craft goods, corn, wool, or, less often, cash, instead of weaving it themselves. By the 1890s men were obtaining unbleached muslin and sewing their own trousers and shirts (Donaldson 1893:41). Some older women made themselves traditional-style mantas and dresses from gingham or calico (Fig. 8), and young girls from government schools sewed commercial cotton into dresses of American style (Udall

Figure 9. Changes in clothing appeared earlier among Hopi men, here wearing American-style clothing in the early 1900s, than among women, who are seen here wearing traditional black blanket-dresses with their commercial cloth mantas. (Courtesy Natural History Museum of Los Angeles County, photo by A. C. Vroman.)

1969:49). Crane (1913:5) estimated that by 1913, thirty percent of the Hopis were dressing like whites (Fig. 9). In the ultraconservative village of Hotevilla, however, some old women were still wearing as their daily apparel the black wool blanket-dress and red belt, without the addition of a European-style underdress, as recently as 1940.

Much of what we know about Hopi clothing in the late 1800s and early 1900s comes from first-hand accounts by Stephen (1936) and from photographs by Wittick, Voth, Hildebrand, Vroman, Mora, and others. Adult women in these photographs wear the blanket-dress and red belt. Striped shoulder blankets and white mantas with blue and red borders are much in evidence (Fig. 10). Children are generally in American dress. Photographs taken around the time of World War I show younger women substituting commercial plaid shawls for the standard black wool manta and wearing cotton dresses beneath the black blanket-dress.

A little weaving was still done at Zuni through the early decades of the twentieth century, but it had almost ceased among the other New Mexico pueblos by 1900. Hopi men continued to weave traditional clothing for ceremonial wear for themselves and other Pueblos. Indeed, much of the weaving at Zuni in the early 1900s may have been done by Hopi men residing in that pueblo (Spier 1924:190). The Rio Grande people, however, were unable to secure enough handwoven Hopi articles to meet their needs and turned increasingly after 1900 to commercial cloth as a base for embroidery and for such items as mantas, kilts, and the black blanket-dress. Many villages grew enough native cotton for ceremonial purposes, but even the Hopis produced too little cotton after about 1900 to meet all the demands of local weavers,

Figure 10. In a photograph taken in the early 1900s, male dancers in a Hopi ceremony wear cotton mantas with blue and red borders. (Courtesy Mennonite Library and Archives, North Newton, Kansas, H. R. Voth Collection.)

Plate 1. This Moqui-pattern serape dating to about 1860 was originally recorded as Hopi but more likely was woven at Zuni. It contains a few barely recognizable lazy lines. The corner tassels are part of a recent repair. 68" x 47". (SAR T.104.)

Plate 2. A geometric motif is seen superimposed on a Moqui pattern blanket from Zuni, about 1875. 74" x 56". (SAR T.641.)

who often had to substitute commercial cotton string for warps and spin cotton batting for wefts. Handspun yarn survived as the basic material for wide-loom wool fabrics, but commercial plied yarn was used for embroidery and, retwisted to make it hard and fine, for warp-faced belts.

After 1880, a few weavers began to make heavy wool rugs for sale to tourists, but the Pueblos never really took advantage of the American market as did the Navajos. The decline in Pueblo weaving after 1880 was one manifestation of a growing tendency for men to abandon traditional economic pursuits in order to take up wage work in the American economy. In New Mexico, Pueblo laborers were first employed building the railroads, and later more and more Pueblo people found work in growing urban centers such as Gallup, Albuquerque, and Santa Fe. Although there were fewer opportunities for wage work among the isolated Hopis, alternative employment had definitely diminished the number of local weavers by the 1930s. Had weaving among the Pueblos been a female rather than a male craft, its fate within the American economy might have been quite different. (For a general discussion of culture change in historic times among the Pueblos, see Spicer [1962] and articles on the various pueblos in the *Handbook of North American Indians,* volume 9 [1979]).

ARTISTIC REVIVALS, 1920 TO 1950, AND CONTEMPORARY TEXTILES

The Anglo interest in Indian arts and crafts that began in the 1920s stemmed from a curiosity about Indian culture that grew up in the late nineteenth century after the closing of the American frontier. Anthropologists had begun studies in the Southwest by 1880; Cushing and Stevenson at Zuni and Stephen at Hopi were soon followed by other field workers. Archaeological investigations by Fewkes, Hewett, and others helped stimulate interest in prehistoric art. Many museums in the United States collected and mounted exhibitions of Indian material culture between 1850 and the First World War, and Indian life and crafts had been shown at the Chicago and St. Louis expositions of 1893 and 1905.

Dorothy Dunn (1968:224–313) has given an excellent account of the growth of interest in southwestern Indian art between 1919 and 1940 under the influence of what she terms the "Santa Fe movement," which was started by Anglo artists and writers in Santa Fe and Taos and led to the formation of the New Mexico Association on Indian Affairs in 1922. This organization helped fight the Bursum bill, which would have taken some sixty thousand acres of land from the Pueblos, and worked to improve health services and economic opportunities for Pueblo Indians. It also encouraged Indian artists by organizing and funding national exhibitions. In the same year, Amelia E. White opened a gallery of American Indian art in New York City. The following year saw the establishment of the Indian Arts Fund in Santa Fe under the direction of Kenneth M. Chapman. This fund, sustained by contributions from private citizens, was used over the ensuing forty-nine years to purchase outstanding examples of southwestern Indian art, which today form most of the collection housed at the School of American Research.

The economic hardships of the Great Depression in the early thirties moved private organizations and government agencies alike to explore ways of helping impoverished Indians earn money by upgrading and adapting traditional crafts for tourist sale. Established under the Department of the Interior, the Indian Arts and Crafts Board sent workers into the field to implement such a program, and the Education Division of the United States Indian Service published a series of eight pamphlets on Indian crafts for the instruction of Indian students (see, for example, Underhill 1944). Public interest in Indian art was fostered by stunning exhibitions mounted by the Indian Arts and Crafts Board at the San Francisco Exposition in 1939 and the Museum of Modern Art in New York City a year later.

In 1933 the Santa Fe Indian School was converted into the Institute of American Indian Art, which became a center for training Indian youths in both Euro-American art forms and traditional crafts. Among the latter were Pueblo embroidery and the weaving of warp-patterned belts.

Because of Anglo ideas about the appropriate sexual division of labor, Pueblo girls had been learning needlework in mission and government schools since the early 1900s. They had used these skills to decorate traditional clothing such as kilts, mantas, and shirts. Now they were encouraged also to embroider pocketbooks, place mats, dresses, and other items for sale to whites. In the late thirties, women of the New Mexico Association on Indian Affairs tried to interest retail stores in the eastern United States in marketing this work, but they met with little success. These women also recognized the Rio Grande artisans' need for suitable material to replace the handwoven fabrics

Figure 11. Men dancing in a Blue Bird Dance at San Ildefonso Pueblo in 1935 wear embroidered kilts and sashes elaborately decorated in "Hopi brocade." The women wear traditional black wool dresses with their commercial silk mantas and cotton underdresses. (Courtesy Museum of New Mexico, photo no. 22687, photo by T. Harmon Parkhurst.)

they no longer made or could obtain in sufficient quantity from Hopi. The Association's annual report for 1932, for example, contains the following note (New Mexico Association on Indian Affairs 1932):

> Bemis bags have always been preferred above all else by the Pueblo women as material for embroidery, but the bags have colored stripes woven in them. When Mr. Bemis was in town we appealed to him, and he had woven and sent to us a generous sample, about 50 yards of material. This is now in the hands of the San Juan women, and will be reported on after trial under the needle. Mr. Bemis was much interested in this new use for bagging, and he may be able to solve this question of suitable material that has faced every person who has wished to encourage this beautiful handicraft.

Two commercial firms also sought to meet Pueblo demands for traditional forms of clothing. Tewa Weavers, a small workshop started in Albuquerque in 1938, employed Isleta men and women to weave black wool mantas and plaid shawls on treadle looms. Only one man was still working at this, sporadically, in 1980, but in 1982 the firm was still supplying black wool mantas to the craft cooperative, *Oke Oweenge,* at San Juan Pueblo and to other Pueblo buyers. Rio Grande Weavers in Santa Fe also produced black or dark blue manta cloth in the 1940s.

Although the reaction of Pueblo women to Mr. Bemis's cloth has not been recorded, the use of commercial rather than handwoven fabrics for ceremonial costumes is now accepted practice in the Rio Grande pueblos. The fabrics are cut to look like blanket-dresses, mantas, kilts, or shirts. An open-weave, white cotton cloth is used for articles to be embroidered. In general, both the stitch and the designs worked on the articles are traditional, with some of the women drawing motifs from Mera's *Pueblo Indian Embroidery* (1943). There is, however, a growing tendency to elaborate upon classic-period embroidery patterns. Sometimes, too, a non-Pueblo stitch is used.

In recent years, border designs on mantas and kilts have been increasingly "faked" by appliquéing to the surface of the garment motifs cut from colored cloth. This technique is sometimes substituted for embroidery on tourist items as well. The origin of appliqué among the Pueblos is obscure. It may be a Zuni invention: nineteenth-century Zuni kachina dolls sometimes wear appliquéd garments, and six early breechcloths from that pueblo have appliquéd end designs. The material in one of these, at the University of Colorado Museum, dates from about 1850 (Joe Ben Wheat, personal communication 1982), and the others, all in the collection of the American Museum of Natural History, were probably made about 1910.

Many handmade articles still appear in New Mexico pueblos on feast days (Fig. 11): black wool mantas, white mantas with red and blue borders, blanket-dresses, embroidered black wool or white cotton mantas, embroidered kilts, red belts, white crocheted shirts and leggings, knit leggings, dance sashes in Hopi brocade, and white braided sashes with heavy fringes (Fig. 12). Some of these, particularly the mantas and kilts, must be heirloom pieces that have

Figure 12. At a 1935 Basket Dance at San Ildefonso Pueblo, only traditional clothing can be seen. The men wear fringed sashes and embroidered cotton kilts, the women, black dresses and mantas. (Courtesy Museum of New Mexico, photo no. 3454, photo by T. Harmon Parkhurst.)

been in use for two generations or more. Very few are still handwoven in the traditional manner, and eventually they will be replaced by commercial cloth replicas.

Of the few traditional articles still manufactured today, red belts and knit leggings are produced by both Navajo and Pueblo women and by Hopi men. One or two women at San Juan Pueblo crochet dance shirts and leggings. A few Hopis produce braided sashes, but many of the fringed white sashes worn by Rio Grande dancers today are woven on belt looms by local Pueblo women.

The real problem for Eastern Pueblo dancers is to secure the dance sashes worn in so many rituals. Although one woman at Jemez makes copies of them in embroidery on commercial cloth, Hopi is still seen by most as the true source for these coveted articles. Because the demand so far exceeds the supply, the cost of the sashes has increased since the late 1970s, and the two halves of a sash may even be sold separately.

Embroidery is the most vital and visually appealing of the Rio Grande Pueblo textile arts today. It is worked not only on traditional articles used as dance costumes but also on church vestments and altar cloths and on a wide variety of items for tourist sale. Women make articles on commission for people in their own or other pueblos, or they sell their work at Indian fairs or through outlets such as Oke Oweenge and the Pueblo Cultural Center in Albuquerque. Since about 1970, women in several New Mexico pueblos have begun to weave Navajo-style blankets on treadle looms. One weaver uses the treadle loom to produce a white cotton open-weave fabric specifically designed for embroidery.

The Anglo presence, in sum, affected the textile arts of the New Mexico Pueblos first by bringing about the virtual demise of loom weaving as a man's skill by the early 1900s and then by fostering the revival of some traditional techniques, notably belt weaving and embroidery, as women's art. The market for Indian crafts since World War II has encouraged the women to produce many items for tourist sale, in addition to traditional articles sold to their own people.

The history of Hopi textiles since the 1920s follows a course somewhat different from that described for the New Mexico Pueblos. Except for some embroidery and knitting by women, weaving has continued to be a man's art centered on the production of traditional items of clothing needed for ceremonial costuming.

The quality of Hopi crafts, including weaving, became the concern of Mary-Russell F. Colton, who started the annual Hopi Craftsman Show at the Museum of Northern Arizona in 1930 as a means of increasing public awareness of Hopi art. Prizes were offered for the best woven articles entered in the show each year. Under Mrs. Colton's direction, the Museum imported long-staple Pima cotton and vegetal indigo for sale to weavers. She also worked to revive the use of traditional vegetal dyes and to introduce new varieties of vegetal dyes (Colton 1965). In the late 1930s, the Museum was able to record the names of 213 weavers, all men, 27 of whom were inactive due to illness or advanced age. Eighty-four were spoken of as good, active weavers, but only one man stated that he made his full living from his loom, all the rest using their weaving to supplement income from other sources. Eight Hopi women were listed as embroiderers, and four knew the art of making rabbit-fur robes.

In the first eleven years (1930–1941) of the Hopi Craftsman Show, Hopi weavers submitted a total of 374 pieces. There were 101 "blankets," presumably rugs made for tourist sale. The remaining 273 pieces were traditional articles of clothing. Some were sold to museums, and a very few went to private individuals. The total income from sales was $1,488, or about $135 per year (Whiting 1941). Obviously, few of the weavers were directing their efforts towards the tourist market or depending for their income on returns from the Craftsman Show. Some of their work in those years was sold to Anglos through trading posts at the Hopi mesas, but it is evident that most of it was designed for and sold to their own Pueblo people, as it had been in earlier times.

In spite of efforts by the Museum of Northern Arizona to encourage traditionalism in the textile arts, Hopi weavers have turned increasingly to the use of commercial materials. In 1981 only one man was still weaving rugs from handspun, vegetal-dyed, wool yarns. Cotton string appears in braids, in wedding robe tassels, and as the warps of loom-woven cotton fabrics. Most of the latter now have wefts of white acrylic yarn rather than cotton. Acrylic yarns have also replaced wool in most belts, embroideries, Hopi brocades, and other articles.

There may be as few as twenty active Hopi weavers today. The number is hard to estimate accurately because there are no records of the numbers of pieces woven for trade, gift, or sale to other Hopis or residents of other pueblos. Eleven men submitted a total of twenty-two pieces to the Hopi Craftsman

Show in July, 1981. The craft shop at Second Mesa had about the same number of articles on sale at that time. Principal products are embroidered cotton kilts, Hopi-brocaded sashes, braided cotton sashes, warp-faced belts, and knitted wool leggings. Plain-weave, white cotton wedding robes are still made for local use; I saw three on looms in Second and Third Mesa villages in June, 1981. The woman's white manta with red and blue borders (Fig. 13), the boy's black and white plaid blanket, and the woman's black wool dress are still made and sometimes offered for sale. A few women embroider Hopi motifs on baby quilts, pot holders, and other items, and the traditional kilt design is embroidered on white commercial cloth shirts or sleeveless jackets to good effect. In recent years a few narrow Hopi-brocaded belts and braided sashes have been made. On the whole, however, little has been done to apply traditional techniques to the production of tourist items.

The future of weaving at Hopi seems tenuous. At present, conservative Hopis sustain the craft by their desire for traditional handwoven fabrics. If they compromise, as most Rio Grande Pueblos have done, and accept the use of commercial fabrics embroidered or otherwise modified to resemble traditional forms, the market for weaving will collapse. Equally threatening is the decreasing number of men who weave, a result of the switch to wage work that often takes men away from their villages to urban centers.

Figure 13. A traditional woman's manta with red and blue borders is part of the costume of this Hopi kachina doll, along with a black dress and a red, warp-patterned belt. Height 15". (SAR 31918/12.)

II

Tools and Materials

FIBERS

Handspun cotton and wool yarns survived through the classic period and into the closing years of the nineteenth century as the basic materials in Pueblo weaving. Cotton, the indigenous fiber, has a symbolic importance that was never attached to the more recently introduced fiber, wool. Its association with clouds links cotton also with kachina supernaturals and rain. It is used to decorate masks, altars, and other ceremonial equipment, and it figures in certain mortuary customs. The Hopis traditionally made a mask of raw cotton to place over the face of a deceased person, with the idea of making the spiritual body light, like a cloud. At Zuni such a mask was placed over the faces of deceased members of the war society, who were to become storm clouds, and at Acoma a medicine man made a crown of cotton for the head of a dead person (Bohrer, in press). It is because they need raw cotton for ritual use that many Pueblos continued to raise a few plants until very recently.

The cotton of the aboriginal Southwest, though it had been introduced from Central America via Mexico, differed in certain respects from its botanical relatives in tropical regions of the New World. Most significantly, it was a variety well adapted to the high altitude and arid conditions of the Colorado Plateau. There it grew as an annual rather than a perennial plant and matured in the remarkably short growing season of 84 to 100 days. The fine, short fibers, not quite an inch long, did not adhere closely to the seeds, which made cleaning the cotton by the hand methods of the Pueblos practical.

Accounts of nineteenth- and early twientieth-century Hopi economic life (for example, Beaglehole 1937) furnish information about the way in which cotton was grown and processed. Planting was done in late May, several seeds being placed together in a hole made by a pointed digging stick. Fields were situated where they would be watered by the runoff from a large area during the seasonal rains and flash floods characteristic of the Southwest. Perhaps because of the short growing season, cotton bolls were not allowed to ripen on the stalk but were gathered before they burst open and were spread on roof tops to dry in the sun. When dry, the fiber with seeds was removed from the pods and stored in the houses until needed.

After its separation from the boll, cotton was cleaned, or "ginned," by removing seeds and dirt particles, and the matted fibers were pulled apart, or carded, and arranged loosely in pads or laps from which they could be drawn out in spinning. According to Beaglehole (1937:43), the Hopis did not process their raw cotton until the winter months, when men turned their attention to weaving. At this time women simply picked the seeds out by hand, saving some for next year's planting and roasting the rest to make a kind of popcorn. After ginning, the fibers were thrown in a heap on a pile of clean sand. A number of men then sat around the pile, beating the cotton very lightly with switches made by binding together at their butt ends three to five slender, flexible rods, each about two feet long. The rods radiated from their bound ends to make a fan-like instrument. Beating converted the cotton into a fluffy mass, and the sand cleaned and whitened the fibers. This was all the "carding" that was done until weavers began to use commercial cards around 1852 (Stephen 1936:1181–82).

A second method of processing was to place unginned raw cotton between the folds of a blanket and beat upon the blanket with the switch. This served to loosen the seeds from the fibers, which attached themselves to the surface of the blanket and were scraped off and arranged by hand into loose laps for spinning.

At Hopi, groups of men generally processed cotton in the kivas. Sometimes their work was accompanied by religious ritual. Stevenson (n.d.:147–151) witnessed such a ritual:

> The writer observed the preparing of cotton for the loom at the Hopi village of Shimopavi [Shongopavi] in 1882. This ceremony, which is

Figure 14. Tools used in spinning and weaving. From top to bottom are one end of a temple or stretcher (M.389d); a spindle (M.348); a long batten or sword (M.389s); a backstrap loom cloth bar (M.348); a small batten for use with a backstrap loom (M.399); a weaving comb (M.398); a weaving pick (M.348); and a pair of cards with wool (M.519). Length of long batten is 34".

strictly religious, must be performed with many prayers. A piece of white commercial cotton cloth was spread upon the floor in the chamber of the high priest (head rain priest) and a disk-shaped bed of sand was laid upon the cotton cloth. Several men headed by the high priest took seats around the sand bed and immediately began to pray. In a short time two men appeared bringing a dressed deerskin with a painting of the sun in the center. . . . The painting was gently deposited upon the sand bed, where it remained while a long prayer was offered by the high priest and was responded to by others in tones too low to be heard by the writer. After the prayer each one seated around the painting sprinkled it with sacred meal and drawing his hand to his mouth inhaled the sacred breath from the living god, as it were, for the sun father was supposed to be present in spirit in the shield. The painting was again sprinkled with sacred meal when it was gently lifted and returned to its resting place by the men who brought it. The process of manipulating the cotton then began. A white cloth containing cotton pods was deposited by the sand bed and each man of the circle began picking the cotton and placing it on the bed. The picked cotton was patted with a willowy rod, some two and a half feet in length with five fingers or prongs wrapped securely to it. Great care has to be observed in the patting of the cotton for the slightest carelessness will cause it to fly. The process is most fatiguing, owing to the peculiar motion of the arm. The better part of a day was required to prepare but a small quantity of cotton for the spindle. . . .

After ginning and carding, cotton fibers are spun into yarn. This is accomplished with the aid of the indigenous stick-and-whorl spindle, called by the Spaniards the *malacate* (Fig. 14). The spindle consists of two parts: a smooth, slender stick varying in length from ten to thirty inches and slightly pointed at one or both ends, and a whorl, or flat wooden disk, affixed to the

Figure 15. A Hopi man spinning with a stick-and-whorl spindle, about 1917. (Courtesy Museum of New Mexico, photo no. 21540.)

shaft nearer one end than the other. In spinning, one tip is fastened to the end of the lap of fibers. The Eastern Pueblos spin the fibers off the longer end of the spindle shaft, resting the tip of the shorter end on the ground or setting it in a small cup. The shaft, kept in motion with the right hand, is rotated against the upper leg, and the whorl helps to maintain momentum. Fibers are drawn from the lap with the fingers of the left hand and are twisted together, the yarn forming between the spindle tip and the left hand. Finished yarn is wrapped around the shaft above the whorl. Hopi men attach unspun fibers to the tip of the short end of the spindle and rotate the long end of the shaft on the right thigh (Fig. 15). Spinning was usually a communal process among the Hopis.

Figure 16. Three types of weaving yarn. From left to right: single-ply z-spun; 2-ply z-spun S-twist; 4-ply z-spun S-twist Germantown yarn.

When it was introduced by the Spaniards, wool was spun in exactly the same manner as cotton. The fibers, however, were first cleansed and aligned with the help of a pair of cards (Fig. 14). A card is an Old World tool consisting of a rectangular board with bent wire teeth on one surface and a handle on one long edge. Fibers are placed on the teeth of one card and combed with the toothed surface of the second card. In the mid-nineteenth century at Hopi, and perhaps earlier in the Rio Grande area, Pueblo weavers began to use cards to prepare cotton as well as wool.

Handspun cotton and wool yarns used in Pueblo weaving are characteristically single-ply z-spun (Fig. 16). This means that the fibers in a yarn all trend in the direction of the center line of the letter z when the yarn is held vertically. Yarns destined for use as warps (see Fig. 19) may be respun two or three times to make them thin, hard, and able to withstand the tension and wear to which they will be subjected on the loom during weaving. Weft yarns are generally more loosely spun and are softer and thicker than warps. Two or more single-ply yarns may be twisted together, usually with an S-twist, to make a heavier yarn for use in selvages and braids or as cordage.

Pueblo weavers in the eighteenth and nineteenth centuries (and possibly in the seventeenth) raveled yarns from commercial cloth principally as a means of getting a good, bright red, though other colors were sometimes raveled as well. Used chiefly in embroidery, raveled yarns were of two general types, as described by Fisher and Wheat (1979:199):

Early raveled yarn (1750–1865) was produced from fine cloth with threads about 0.35 mm in diameter, dyed red with lac or cochineal.

Both Z- and S-spun yarns were used until about 1825, after which S-spun dominates until about 1865. Until 1821, the cloth raveled came through Mexico or was produced locally, but by 1826, virtually all cloth came over the Santa Fe Trail, and much of it appears to have been American in origin. Because of their fineness, yarns were usually used paired or tripled, laid parallel to each other and not plied.

Late raveled yarn (1865–1875) is usually termed *American flannel*. Almost all was raveled from wool cloths or blankets, and tends to be fuzzy and soft. Some of the earlier cloths were presumably dyed with cochineal or lac, but most were synthetic-dyed in various shades of orange-red. The yarns are highly variable in diameter, ranging from 0.30 mm to 1.10 mm with most either 0.50 or 0.90 mm, which reflects the wide variety of fabrics being raveled. The smallest were used in groups of three to five, and sometimes as bundles with as many as nine threads. Intermediate sized yarns might be used paired or as singles, while larger yarns were used as singles.

Early raveled yarns are generally referred to in the literature as *bayeta*. It was thought that they were raveled from English baize, a term for which bayeta is the Spanish equivalent. Since these yarns are, in fact, varied in source and appearance, it seems better to describe them simply by their physical characteristics.

A third type of yarn used to some extent by the Pueblos between 1865 and 1880, although more characteristic of Navajo weaving, was made from cloth that did not ravel easily into separate yarns but was pulled apart as fibers instead. These were recarded and respun into a single-ply yarn. Usually the yarn is pink, as red commercial fibers were carded with white native wool.

Still another use made in late classic times of red cloth that raveled poorly was to cut the cloth into narrow strips and weave these in as wefts.

The commercial materials that gradually replaced handspun and raveled yarns after 1870 are not difficult to recognize. White cotton string, used first as warps in wide-loom fabrics and belts and later in white dance sashes, is multiple-ply, usually with a final S-twist. Early commercial wool yarns were three-ply, but those used since 1875 are four-ply, S-twist, synthetic-dyed—the type generally called Germantown after the town in Pennsylvania where it was originally produced. Cotton batting, which appears as weftage in twentieth-century Hopi fabrics, is very loosely handspun, soft, and thick.

When documentation of the age of a textile is lacking, as is usually the case in museum collections, its approximate date of manufacture and its provenience can often be determined by examining the types of yarn it contains.

DYES

Although Hopi formulas for a wide range of colors were recorded by Colton (1965), I have seen only four native dyes on traditional Pueblo textiles: yellow, brownish-red, black, and purple. Indigo, derived from a Mexican plant of unknown species, was imported into the Southwest in lump form by the seventeenth-century Spaniards to be traded to Pueblo weavers. It became their most versatile and popular dye, yielding a stunning range of blues and, in combination with yellow, subtle greens. There is no firm evidence that the Anasazi ancestors of the Pueblos had indigo dye, although it was probably known to Hohokam and Salado weavers in southern Arizona and to the Mogollon of southwestern New Mexico.

According to Colton (1965:37–49), yellow dyes were extracted from a number of different native plants. Black was made by combining tannin from the seeds of the black-seeded Indian sunflower *(Helianthus* sp.) or the leaves and small branches of sumac *(Rhus trilobata)* with a water-soluble black powder made by cooking crushed yellow ocher with melted piñon gum, allowing the mixture to cool and harden, and grinding it fine on a stone mortar (Colton 1965:82–85). It was usually applied to natural black or brown wool to intensify the color. The source of the brownish-red found on early eighteenth-century wool and cotton fragments has not been determined, although it is known to be a plant dye. Purple was extracted from purple corn for use in a number of ceremonial contexts: to dye a young boy's first handspun cotton kilt, as a body paint, and as a paint for ceremonial wooden objects (Colton 1965:59; Wright 1979:13).

The technique of preparing indigo with stale human urine probably accompanied the dye into the Southwest. In this process, urine is collected in a large pottery jar that

Figure 17. A Hopi man photographed in 1901 weaves a black wool manta on an upright loom. One border and a portion of the center have been completed, the weaving reversed on the loom, and the second border and part of the midsection of the manta woven. The man wears traditional cotton pants and a breechcloth. (Courtesy Museum of New Mexico, photo no. 37706, photo by William H. Simpson.)

Figure 18. Stefanita Herrera of Cochiti Pueblo poses with a finished Navajo-style belt on a backstrap loom, about 1935. She uses a Hopi-style belt to strap the cloth bar to her waist. (Courtesy Museum of New Mexico, photo no. 2288, photo by T. Harmon Parkhurst.)

is sealed and placed in a warm room for several days while the urine ferments. A double handful of indigo lumps is then added to the liquid, and the yarn is put in and allowed to soak for two to four days, depending on the intensity of the blue color desired. The liquid actually has a greenish color at this point, but when the yarn is removed from the jar and placed in the sun it oxidizes to blue. Colton (1965:50–51) states "Of all the dyes used by the Hopi, indigo is the most precious to him. It is the sacred color of the sky. The Hopi name, *saqwa,* is used to mean blue, of the sky, the precious turquoise, and the blue of flowers, birds and butterflies. Next to turquoise, it is the most precious thing that he might possess." In spite of their value, cloths dyed with indigo or any other color in which urine was used were felt to be offensive to the gods and could not be utilized in certain ceremonies (Stephen 1936:82).

The early raveled red yarns used in classic period pieces were colored with natural dyes—cochineal, lac, and possibly madder. Lac, an insect dye of great antiquity in India, was used in nineteenth-century American and English mills. It has been identified as the dye source in the raveled red embroidery yarns on the breechcloth illustrated in Plate 19 and in the brownish-red yarns, apparently handspun, in a second breechcloth (Pl. 18). The latter finding is curious, as there are no records of the importation of lac as a dyestuff into the Southwest.

Cochineal, a New World insect dye, was imported to some extent into the Southwest from Mexico by the Spaniards. It may have been made available to Pueblo weavers, and it is reported to have been used at Acoma in the 1740s (Joe Ben Wheat, personal communication 1982). However, no handspun, cochineal-dyed yarns have so far been identified in Pueblo textiles.

Synthetic-dyed commercial yarns and the dyes themselves began to replace handspun yarns and natural dyes during the late classic period. The literature on southwestern textiles usually calls these dyes *anilines,* meaning

Figure 19. (a) Detail showing how string loops pass around alternate warps and are fastened to the slender heddle stick. Pulling the stick brings these warps forward. Shed rod above heddle passes behind other warp set, forcing it forward when the shed rod is brought down to the heddle loops. (b) The formation of two sheds in plain weave. (1) The string-loop heddle is pulled, bringing the striped warp set forward. The batten holds the triangular space thus created, that is, the shed, open for passage of the weft, x. (2) The shed rod is forced down against the string loops, pushing forward all black wefts and forming a second shed through which the second weft, y, will pass. (c) Detail of notched end of temple extending from behind the warps. The large arrow points to its actual position. (1) The wooden pin will be passed through the edge of the completed fabric, as shown by the small arrow. (2) The pin in position, its tip forced through the cloth. It lies in the groove of the temple and is lashed to it behind the fabric. As weaving progresses, the temple is moved up so as to be just below the work area.

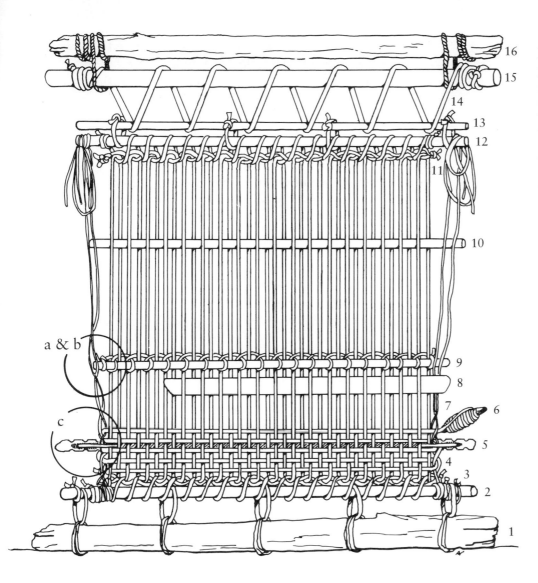

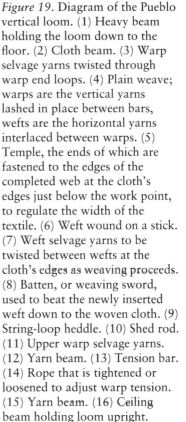

Figure 19. Diagram of the Pueblo vertical loom. (1) Heavy beam holding the loom down to the floor. (2) Cloth beam. (3) Warp selvage yarns twisted through warp end loops. (4) Plain weave; warps are the vertical yarns lashed in place between bars, wefts are the horizontal yarns interlaced between warps. (5) Temple, the ends of which are fastened to the edges of the completed web at the cloth's edges just below the work point, to regulate the width of the textile. (6) Weft wound on a stick. (7) Weft selvage yarns to be twisted between wefts at the cloth's edges as weaving proceeds. (8) Batten, or weaving sword, used to beat the newly inserted weft down to the woven cloth. (9) String-loop heddle. (10) Shed rod. (11) Upper warp selvage yarns. (12) Yarn beam. (13) Tension bar. (14) Rope that is tightened or loosened to adjust warp tension. (15) Yarn beam. (16) Ceiling beam holding loom upright.

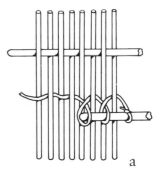

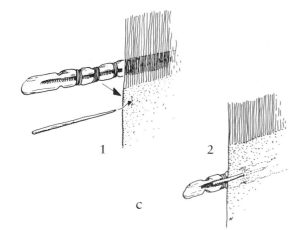

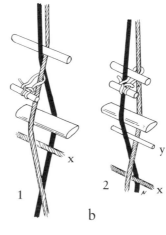

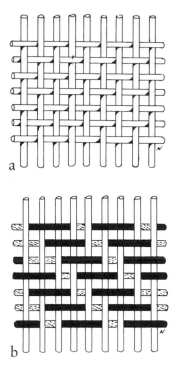

a

b

Figure 20. Plain and twill weaves. (a) Plain weave, wefts interlacing over one warp, under one warp. (b) Balanced 2/2 diagonal twill, the weft interlacing over two warps, under two warps. Each successive weft will be inserted one warp set to the right or left of the preceding weft.

that they are coal tar derivatives. Since most no longer are, I prefer the general term synthetic.

Few of the dyes in Pueblo textiles have been chemically tested. (The results of dye tests run on eight pieces from the School of American Research collection are given in the Appendix.) Usually one estimates the date of a yarn by its physical characteristics and then assumes that the dye is of the type commonly in use at that date. One can feel fairly confident in most cases in calling a dye either natural or synthetic on this basis, but the exact source of a natural dye remains in question. Saltzman's (1979:212–16) recent analysis of dyes in Rio Grande colonial blankets proves that no one can name the source of a dye simply by looking at a colored yarn and that many of our assumptions about dye sources in eighteenth- and nineteenth-century textiles are incorrect. Saltzman found no brazilwood, logwood, or mountain mahogany, for example, all of which were assumed to have been popular Spanish dyes. His finding that lac was an important dye in early nineteenth-century Hispanic pieces agrees with Wenger's analyses (see Appendix) of dyes on raveled yarns in Pueblo textiles, refuting the generally held assumption that all natural reds were cochineal.

LOOMS AND WEAVING TOOLS

Two types of looms have been used by the historic Pueblos, an upright loom for wide fabrics and brocaded dance sashes (Fig. 17) and a backstrap loom for belts (Fig.18). These are the same indigenous forms on which prehistoric weavers made the cotton fabrics found in southwestern archaeological sites.

The warp yarn is prepared for the wide, upright loom (Fig. 19) by winding it continuously between two poles set parallel to one another about six inches above the ground and as far apart as the proposed length of the warp. Three two-ply yarns are then twined through the warp loops on the outside of the poles. These help to space the warps evenly and to hold them in position. They remain on the finished fabric as warp selvage yarns. Next, warping poles are removed. One end of the warp is bound to the cloth beam, the other end to the yarn beam. The warp is then fastened in upright position between permanently fixed ceiling and floor beams. Warp tension is adjusted by tightening or loosening the rope that fastens the yarn beam to the ceiling beam.

Plate 3. A combination of Rio Grande, Navajo, and Pueblo characteristics, the presence of silvery-gray yarns, and the thick, loosely spun wefts all suggest that this serape was woven at Zuni in the 1870s. 66" x 45". (SAR T.77.)

Plate 4. The blue in this Zuni blanket from about 1870 is indigo, and the red yarns were raveled from commercial synthetic-dyed cloth. 66" x 49". (SAR T.323.)

Plate 5. The "pinching in" of color bands on this unique serape, which dates to about 1880, was accomplished by forcing wefts down tightly with the weaving fork and filling in the resulting curves with white wefts in tapestry weave. The loose weave and low yarn count suggest Pueblo manufacture. 53" x 43". (SAR T.347.)

Before weaving begins, cords (usually three two-ply) are loosely fastened at each edge of the warp. These will be incorporated into the cloth as weft selvage yarns during weaving, twining about each other between every two or three passages of weft.

Warps are divided into sets, each set controlled by a shed rod or a string-loop heddle. For plain weave (Fig. 20a) there are two sets of warps, for twill weaves, three, four, or more sets (Fig. 20b). The weft, wound on a slender stick, is passed through the triangular space, or shed, created between warp sets when a heddle is pulled forward. It is forced down into position with a fork (formerly made of wood but nowadays consisting of a regular table fork) or with a small wooden pick (see Fig. 14) and beaten against the weft below it with the batten, or weaving sword. As the piece is woven, the width of the textile is maintained with the help of a temple, a flat, slender measuring stick, the ends of which are pinned at the edges of the web just below the newly inserted weft picks (Fig. 19c).

Wefts are inserted from the cloth beam upward towards the center. When a border, or a narrow width of fabric, has been completed, the yarn and cloth bars are released from ceiling and floor supports, and the entire warp set is reversed, or turned upside-down (see Fig. 17). The woven section is now at the top of the loom. Weaving resumes, beginning from the lower bar and continuing upward. There will be short lengths of unused weft selvage yarns at the edges of the fabric where upper and lower portions of the weave meet. These yarns are fashioned into small tassels or braids. Relatively small, plain-weave serapes or rugs need not be reversed on the loom during weaving.

In recent years, belts have been woven on warps wound around two poles that are then fastened between the upper and lower bars of the regular verti-

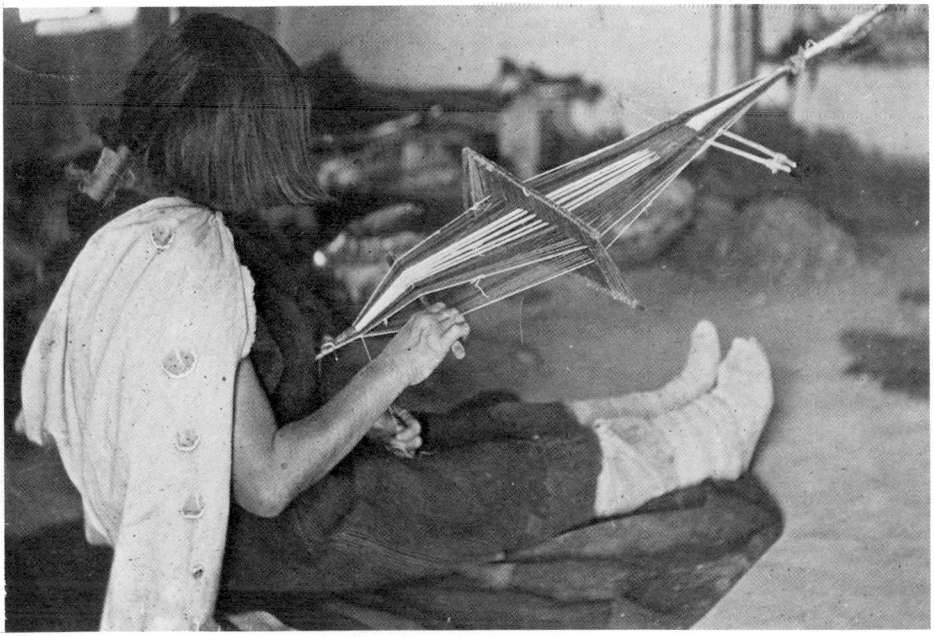

Figure 21. This Zuni woman uses a hole-and-slot heddle in weaving a belt on a backstrap loom. Even-numbered warps pass through holes at the center of each reed in the heddle; odd-numbered warps pass through slots between the reeds. When the heddle is pulled down, even-numbered warps are on the lower plane and one shed is formed. Raising the heddle lifts them above odd-numbered warps to form the second shed. The weaver wears a black dress embroidered in indigo blue. (Courtesy Museum of New Mexico, photo no. 86939, photo by Bartlelmess and Schofield.)

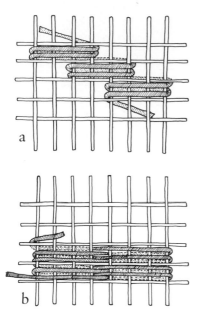

Figure 22. Two prehistoric embroidery stitches that were inserted parallel to the wefts: (a) wrap-stitch; (b) double running stitch.

cal loom. Nineteenth- and early twentieth-century weavers, however, used the backstrap loom. It consists of two rods about eighteen to twenty-eight inches long, to which warps are bound in the same manner as for the vertical loom. One rod, the cloth bar (see Fig. 14), is fastened to a strap that runs behind the weaver's back as he or she sits on the ground (see Fig. 18). The yarn beam is fastened to a tree, a wall, or even the weaver's feet as he sits with outstretched legs. The weaver regulates warp tension with his body. Some nineteenth- and early twentieth-century Pueblo weavers used the European hole-and-slot heddle (Fig. 21) with the backstrap loom, but this innovation was discarded in favor of the indigenous shed rod and string-loop heddle later in the twentieth century.

EMBROIDERY

Embroidery—the decoration of cloth by inserting yarns with a needle—graces many classic period textiles, including Zuni and Acoma black wool mantas, white cotton mantas, white cotton shirts, breechcloths, and kilts.

Embroidery was not a common technique in the Southwest before A.D. 1400, if the archaeological record can be trusted. Anasazi Pueblo sites dating between A.D. 1100 and 1300 have yielded fragments of cloth decorated by running-stitch embroidery in simple line patterns, usually simulating diamond or diagonal twill weave. The only complex embroidered designs come from two Sinagua sites (A.D. 1100–1300) in the Verde Valley of central Arizona and from the Salado ruins in Tonto National Monument (A.D. 1250–1400) in southern Arizona. These are fragments of plain-weave, white cotton cloth embroidered in white, brown, light blue, or dark blue-green cotton yarns (Kent 1983). The embroidery appears to have been oriented along the border of the cloth—a manta, perhaps, or the end of a sash. One fragment is unique in bearing a pattern worked in four colors on a gauze-weave foundation. Two kinds of stitches were used in these pieces: wrap-stitch and double running stitch (Fig. 22), both of which lie parallel to the wefts.

Embroidery yarns were probably threaded to a needle of some sort, perhaps a yucca leaf tip of the type found in many archaeological sites. Always inserted between warp and weft, the needle never split a yarn. Stitches were

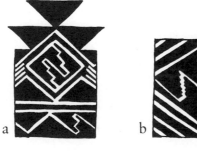

Figure 23. Similar prehistoric and historic designs using interlocking terraced triangles worked in negative patterning. (a) Black and white embroidery on a cotton manta, Acoma, about 1875. (b) Brown and white slit tapestry band, northern Arizona, about 1200. (Drawing by Julie Wagner.)

completely regular in length; that is, the yarn consistently crossed an established number of warps (usually two, four, or six) on each passage. Design motifs were very similar to those seen in contemporary embroidery (Fig. 23). Narrow lines of the background fabric were allowed to show between the embroidered elements of a pattern, forming what has been called a negative design, an outstanding characteristic of Pueblo embroidery today.

Embroidery apparently increased in importance as a decorative technique in late prehistoric times. Murals in the Hopi country, painted during the century just preceding the Spanish conquest, depict kilts with border designs that probably represent embroidery. As mentioned earlier, embroidery became even more important as a decorative technique in historic times, replacing pre-Spanish decorative weave techniques.

Oddly enough, the stitch employed historically is entirely unlike that found on prehistoric material, and its use has not been documented for European work either. Historic Pueblo stitches parallel warps rather than wefts. In classic period pieces, a pair of handspun or raveled yarns was used, often twisted together between insertions of the needle. The needle passed down through the cloth, back under one or two wefts, and up between the two embroidery yarns (Fig. 24). In contemporary embroidery, a single four-ply commercial yarn is used, and the needle is passed between the plies as it is brought to the surface. The Pueblo stitch can effectively create large areas of solid color on the surface of the cloth.

Other stitches, including outline, satin, overcast and herringbone, are used today in limited ways in certain parts of an embroidery design. Contemporary workers sometimes use a regular embroidery hoop to stretch the cloth in the work area. Formerly, two flat wooden pins were fastened in the cloth, parallel to one another and about six inches apart, to hold a small area of cloth flat for stitching (Fig. 25). According to Hough (1918:260), a temple was also used at times to stretch a manta border for embroidering.

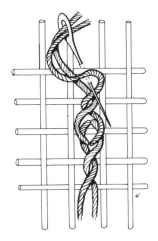

Figure 24. The historic Pueblo embroidery stitch.

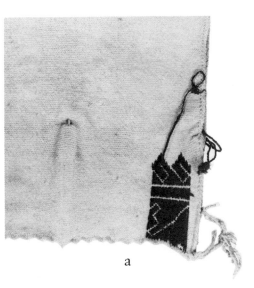

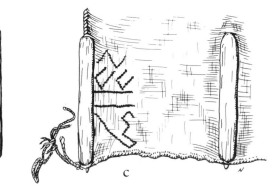

Figure 25. The use of embroidery pins. (a) Partially completed Hopi kilt border showing embroidery pins inserted to hold the fabric flat (courtesy Department of Anthropology, Smithsonian Institution). (b) Embroidery pin, 6 1/8" long. (c) Reverse side of kilt border with pins in place. (b and c after Hough 1918:Fig. 37b).

a   b   c

Figure 26. In a Hopi village in the early 1900s, men wear the traditional Pueblo striped blankets. (Courtesy Mennonite Library and Archives, North Newton, Kansas, H. R. Voth Collection.)

The Textiles

III

Traditional textiles served a variety of functions in everyday and ceremonial Pueblo life. They can be grouped into ten categories according to use and style: serapes and rugs; men's shoulder blankets; women's mantas; men's shirts; kilts; breechcloths; fringed white sashes; leggings; belts, garters, and hair ties; and rabbit-fur robes.

Each category is discussed in this chapter in terms not only of its stylistic and technical features but also of its history and relationship to prehistoric forms. When possible, the significance of a given textile type within Pueblo culture is recorded. Information on this point is scarce for the New Mexico Pueblos. Considering, however, that at Zuni certain textiles were demanded as partial indemnity for crimes against the person (Smith and Roberts 1954: 52–58), it is probably safe to assume that textiles were symbolically and economically as valuable in the New Mexico towns as Wright (1979:11) reports them to be at Hopi:

> The giving of clothing among the Hopi had, before the introduction of manufactured goods, been ritualized into complex patterns. Social and ceremonial obligations between both individuals and clans were marked by such gifts. Articles of clothing were given to individuals at birth and when they reached some milestone in their lives such as initiation, puberty, or marriage. The assumption of a particular piece of clothing indicated passage from one social state to another. . . .
>
> In addition to being markers of age and sex there were parts of clothing that marked the induction of the Hopi into societies or ritual

Figure 27. The "open" corner on a Hopi manta (bottom), with selvage yarns loosely tied at some distance from the fabric, is contrasted with a typical Navajo corner treatment. In the latter, warp and weft selvage yarns are knotted together at the corner, and extra yarns are run through the fabric to form a small tassel. (Manta, SAR T.117; Navajo blanket, SAR T.46.)

groups. Still other items of clothing were worn only by individuals who performed specific duties. Regardless of the age of a person who dies, the attire he was buried in would indicate to the inhabitants of the Underworld his exact social and ceremonial standing, just as it did in the real world.

Additional evidence of the value placed on textiles is the practice at Hopi, and perhaps other pueblos, of purposely slashing the clothing in which a person was buried, in order to deter grave-robbing (Stephen 1936:825).

Following the descriptions of traditional Pueblo textiles in this chapter, a few typical pieces from the European-Pueblo tradition are illustrated and briefly annotated.

SERAPES AND RUGS

The term *serape* refers to the long, narrow, weft-faced woolen blankets woven by the Pueblos as the result of Spanish influence and used as both wearing and bed blankets. Two types of serapes were produced in the eighteenth and nineteenth centuries. The first, popularly called the "Moqui-pattern" serape, was tightly woven from fine-spun yarns in narrow weft stripes alternately of indigo blue and black, sometimes relieved by lines of white (Pl. 1). It seems to have been reserved for wear on "best" occasions. The term *Moqui*, an alternative name once used for the Hopi people, was applied by dealers to this serape style, which they assumed to be Hopi-woven. Called the "Spanish pelt" by the Navajos, the pattern was probably introduced into the Southwest by the Spaniards along with indigo dye and wool. It was common to Navajo, Pueblo, and Rio Grande Hispanic weaving alike. After the mid-nineteenth century, elaborate geometric designs were often superimposed on Moqui-pattern blankets (Pl. 2).

The second type of serape served as an ordinary, everyday wearing blanket. Loosely woven of rather coarse yarns, this type was patterned by broad bands of colored stripes alternating with bands of natural gray, brown, or white (Plates 3, 4, and 5). Photographs taken at Hopi around the turn of the century show most men wearing blankets of this second type, almost always with the design bands in vertical position (Fig. 26). American-made blankets are

Figure 28. The weft edge of this Zuni blanket shows four pairs of warps but no extra selvage yarns. (SAR T.641.)

also in evidence, but there are very few Moqui-pattern serapes. The impression is that the Moqui style, traditional since early Spanish days, had all but disappeared by 1900.

Since both types of serapes were woven by nineteenth-century Hispanics, Navajos, and Pueblos, one is faced with finding ways to differentiate the work of these three groups. There are several clues that help in identifying Pueblo pieces (Kent, in press). Pueblo blankets tend to be wider in relation to their length than the average Navajo or Spanish blanket, and Pueblo weavers did not batten their wefts as tightly as did Navajo weavers. The average yarn count for Pueblo blankets is 3-5 warps and 10-20 wefts to the inch, whereas that for Navajo blankets is 6-12 warps and 20-100 wefts per inch (Wheat 1979:31). Warp and weft selvages on Pueblo blankets are typically composed of three two-ply yarns, whereas the usual Navajo selvage consists of two three-ply yarns. The unused ends of selvage yarns are not usually tied tightly together in Pueblo blankets and mantas, as they are in Navajo pieces, but may be loosely knotted or braided together an inch or so beyond the corner of the finished piece (Fig. 27). Lazy lines, the diagonal breaks in the weave that characterize Navajo work, seldom appear in Pueblo blankets. These lines result from the Navajo practice of sequentially filling in limited sections of the warp

Figure 29. Collected at Zuni in 1895 by Col. Frank Grygla, this rug has a geometric design in brown, blue, red, yellow, and white. 74" x 60". (SAR T.309.)

rather than carrying each pick of weft from edge to edge of the web as is normal Pueblo practice.

In weaving large shoulder blankets, Navajo women often reversed their warps on the loom and wove from both ends towards the center, Pueblo fashion. Usually, however, they worked the unused ends of the weft selvage yarns back into the fabric, rather than making them into edge tassels as the Pueblos did. Navajo weavers also solved differently the problem of keeping the work area within convenient reach when making women's dresses and most serapes and rugs. They would release and lower the yarn beam after completing a portion of the web, then fold the woven section on itself and sew its upper edge tightly to the cloth bar. This process left a row of small, puckered holes in the finished piece, a feature not characteristic of Pueblo blankets or rugs.

Zuni blankets conform to these general guidelines less often than those of other pueblos. Zuni weavers often treated selvages according to Navajo practice, using two three-ply or two-ply yarns. Blankets from Zuni may also have lazy lines, and at least one Zuni weaver is described by Spier (1924:186) as not only reversing her work on the loom but also lowering the yarn beam and sewing the completed section of the blanket to the cloth beam.

Occasionally one finds a Zuni blanket with a weft edge devoid of selvage yarns, the weft simply passing around paired or tripled outer warps on each passage (Fig. 28). Sometimes, too, an inch or so of warp will be left unfilled at the ends of a blanket and twisted into a fringe (Pl. 3). These features are characteristic of fabrics made on Spanish treadle looms.

Spier (1924:187), in his description of blanket weaving at Zuni in 1916, reported a practice not noted for other southwestern weavers, which would produce a distinctive weft edge: "A length of weft slightly greater than the width of warps is broken from the ball of yarn. This is carried through the shed with the fingers and picked very slack for about a foot at a time. The sword beats down. The surplus weft at the edges is turned back into the fell." Perhaps this was idiosyncratic behavior on the part of the weaver observed by Spier. I have not noted such weft edges on Zuni blankets I have studied.

Hopis, Zunis, and some other Pueblos after 1880 began to weave rugs of the same shape and design as serapes and technically identical to them (Fig. 29). Made for sale to tourists, these rugs are of coarse, heavy yarns intended to withstand use on the floor. Pueblo serapes and rugs of the late nineteenth and early twentieth centuries are not generally as innovative in design and

Plate 6. This rug was woven from natural and synthetic-dyed handspun wool yarns by the Hopi weaver, Qoyawayma, at Oraibi in 1927. 60" x 43½". (SAR T.498.)

Plate 7. In a typical Hopi rug woven between 1930 and 1950, the pattern of blue and brown stripes with beaded edges is reminiscent of nineteenth-century Moqui-pattern blankets. 62" x 42½". (SAR T.564.)

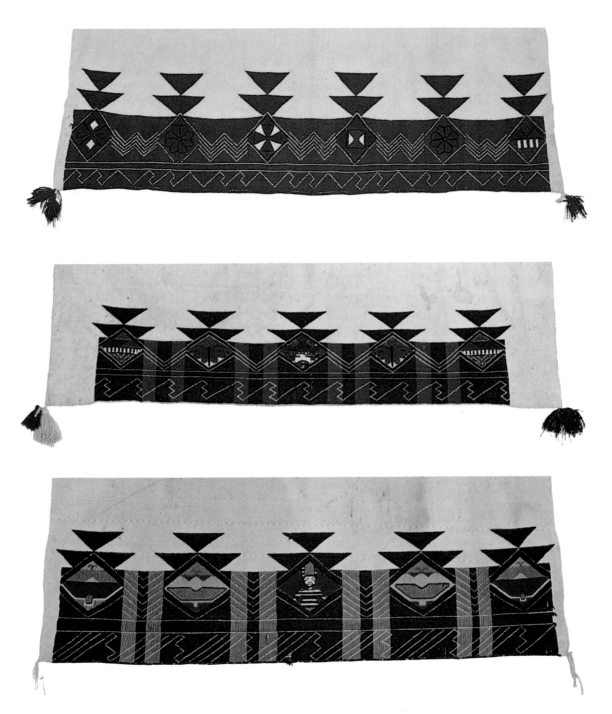

Plate 8. Three plain-weave cotton mantas, probably woven at Hopi, have embroidered border designs that could have been added in other pueblos. Top to bottom: SAR T.42, Zuni, 1920s, 59" wide; SAR T.73, Santo Domingo, 1930; SAR T.404, about 1930.

Plate 9. Purchased at Zuni in 1926, this manta was recorded as a Shalako robe. Motifs within the lower border represent a sunflower and a rainbow-cloud-lightning-rain symbol. Blue, red, yellow, and white are the colors Zunis find beautiful. 60" x 72". (SAR T.11.)

Plate 10. On a white, handspun cotton manta with raveled red embroidery yarns, two "birds" below the upper border identify the piece as coming from Acoma Pueblo. The natural red dye dates the piece to the mid-1800s. 42" x 52". (Laboratory of Anthropology 9038/12.)

color use as those woven by Navajos. Pueblo men preferred to weave variations of stripe patterns, although they were fully as capable as Navajo women of producing complex tapestry designs, and some of them did so. Stevenson (1904:372–73) recorded two instances at Zuni:

> In 1881 a young boy about 12 years of age became jealous over the writer's admiration for the Navaho blankets and determined to see what he could do. Going to work with no design before him, he produced a saddle blanket of exceptional beauty. The elaborate figures were woven in various colors on a red ground. In 1902 a Zuni priest presented the writer with a blanket of his own weaving, which, though not fine, was elaborate in design and color. It was made in order to show the writer that the Zunis possess the art of weaving blankets in the Navaho style even though they do not practice it. They prefer to purchase blankets of the more elaborate kind from the Navahos and give their time to other things.

In the early 1900s, Fred Harvey employed Hopi men to weave Navajo-style rugs at the Hopi House at Grand Canyon (James 1927:164). Whiting (1969–78) describes a picture postcard purchased about 1937 showing what is purported to be a Hopi Indian weaver working in a non-native setting (possibly the Grand Canyon) on a textile featuring a kachina mask and rain clouds on a white field.

By 1930, the weaving of rugs and blankets had ceased in all the pueblos except Hopi (Pl. 6). Under the influence of the Museum of Northern Arizona, several Hopi men revitalized the art with a new emphasis on natural wool tones, indigo blue, and a range of newly-developed vegetal dyes in place of synthetic colors. Many of their rug patterns clearly drew inspiration from classic Moqui-pattern wearing blankets (Pl. 7).

Figure 30. A boy's plain-weave, natural brown and white blanket, made between about 1890 and 1910. 24" x 37½". (SAR T.436.)

Figure 31. A Hopi infant wrapped in a plaid blanket and placed on a cradle board, about 1895 or 1900. (Courtesy California Historical Society/Title Insurance and Trust Company [Los Angeles] Collection of Historical Photographs.)

HOPI PLAID SHOULDER BLANKETS

In early historic times there apparently were several types of men's shoulder blankets shaped like women's mantas, or wider than long when width is measured along the wefts. It may be that each Pueblo (or possibly each language group, such as Tewa, Keres, or Hopi) originally had its own style. Zuni men wore very large, coarse, plain-weave, black wool blankets. Because these were replaced by commercial blankets after 1890 and because they were used as burial shrouds, very few found their way into museum collections (Douglas 1940c:185). Isleta men are said to have had thin, solid blue blankets that were also used as burial shrouds. None has survived (Douglas 1939:164).

Until recently, Hopi weavers made blankets and rugs of the type commonly known as the Navajo "chief blanket," patterned by black and white weft stripes with wide design bands along the top and bottom edges and at the center. There is no record that the Pueblos have used these kinds of textiles as shoulder blankets since the end of the nineteenth century.

The only shoulder blanket to survive in its traditional form is the plaid blanket of the Hopis (Fig. 30). Woven of black and white or brown and white wool, a few are still made for infants and small boys today (Fig. 31). Tradi-

Figure 32. A fragment of cotton plaid cloth in red and white plain weave, from the Verde Valley Salt Mine in central Arizona, about 1300. Width about 5". (Courtesy Arizona State Museum, The University of Arizona, photo by E. B. Sayles.)

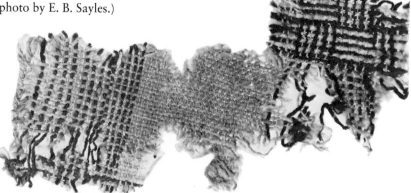

tion has it that these were of cotton before the Spaniards arrived with their sheep, and the belief is supported by finds of prehistoric fragments of plaid and check-patterned textiles. Pieces of brown and white and dark blue and white plain-weave plaid come from Tonto National Monument (A.D. 1250–1400) in southern Arizona, and bits of red and white plaid come from a site of the same age in the Verde Valley (Fig. 32). There is a fragment of brown and white plaid, woven in an irregular twill, from Los Guanacos (A.D. 700–1100) in the Salt River Valley. Brown and white checked plain-weave cloth was found in a Pueblo I (A.D. 700–900) burial in Tsegi Canyon in northern Arizona and at the Canyon Creek site (A.D. 1200–1400) in central Arizona; and a red and white check comes from Ventana Cave, a Desert Hohokam site (A.D. 1000–1400). So far as can be determined, the weaving of check and plaid patterns survived into historic times only among the Hopis.

It is said to have been the custom at Hopi for a man to wear a plaid shoulder blanket at that point in the wedding ceremony when his bride received her new clothing (Whiting 1969–78), and he is supposed to have been buried in the blanket at death (Stephen 1936:825). Traditionally, only natural white, black, or brown wool could be used for plaid blankets, as black dyes had to be boiled, and articles containing boiled dye could not be taken by the dead to the next world (Douglas 1940b:178).

In spite of their alleged cultural importance, there is little actual documentation for men's use of plaid blankets within the last hundred years. A single photograph taken at Mishongnovi in 1902 by A. C. Vroman (Webb and Weinstein 1973:105) shows a man wrapped in what may be a native-woven plaid blanket. In the School of American Research collection, there are two photographs taken by Henry R. Voth, again from the early 1900s, of

Figure 33. A boy's plaid blanket woven in reversed twill pattern, about 1930. 27" x 30". (SAR T.663.)

male dancers wearing what appear to be plaid kilts, perhaps boys' blankets reused as ceremonial costumes.

Apparently, Pueblo-woven plaid shoulder blankets were discarded in favor of American-made products that became available toward the end of the nineteenth century. This does not mean, however, that adult-size plaid blankets were no longer woven by the Hopis. Thirty large, handsome examples were entered as sale items in the Craftsman Show between 1930 and 1941. The number woven each year since then has decreased, and to my knowledge none has been produced since the early 1970s. Blankets woven since the 1930s contain more black than earlier pieces, and the yarn is dyed, not natural.

Hopi weavers still make a few small plaid blankets of the size traditionally given to infants and boys. Those seen for sale in the last three years were woven of acrylic yarn and bore only a slight resemblance to the older woolen pieces.

It was the custom on Third Mesa for a father or grandfather to make a small, simply designed plaid blanket for a baby within its first twenty days of life (Titiev 1944:195–96). As the child grew, he or she was given several different blankets of larger size and increasing complexity of design, not necessarily plaids. When the child reached the age of eight or nine years, a more elaborate blanket was presented. For a girl this was a small version of the woman's white manta with blue and red borders; for a boy it was a plaid blanket (Fig. 33). Titiev (1944:387) noted that a boy might appear in such a blanket at the formal wedding ceremony of his parents if the wedding had been delayed for several years after they in fact became husband and wife.

Plaid blankets were woven on the regular vertical loom and were either square or, like women's mantas, wider than long. Very small blankets might

Figure 34. Black yarns in this handsome, diamond twill, man's blanket are dyed, probably with synthetic dye. Dating to 1931, it was woven at Hopi for sale to tourists. The broad center stripe is reminiscent of "chief blanket" patterning. 46" x 62". (Laboratory of Anthropology 9086/12.)

be plain weave or diagonal twill with simple designs, but adult-size examples often have extraordinarily complex patterns that would have been difficult both to plan and to execute (Fig. 34). They require four controls, three heddles, and a shed rod strung for 2/2 diagonal or reversed twill (see Fig. 20) or for diamond or herringbone twill (see Fig. 42). In weaving these blankets, the warps were reversed on the loom after a yard or so was completed. In some plaid blankets, warp borders are diamond twill and center portions diagonal twill, which means that heddles had to be restrung after the borders were completed.

The design on a weft-faced serape or rug must be carried by the wefts alone, since the warps will not be visible in the finished piece. In open-weave plaid and check blankets, however, warps and wefts are of equal importance to the design. A weaver strings the warps on the loom in alternating black and white bands that vary in width according to the planned pattern. Black

Figure 35. A Hopi bride wears a white cotton wedding manta and carries a second manta and a fringed sash in her reed "suitcase." (Courtesy Museum of Northern Arizona.)

Figure 36. A Hopi wedding manta and reed carrying case probably made in the 1920s. Notice the braid ties at the upper edge of the manta, the simple tassels at the upper corners, and the complex cylindrical tassels at the lower corners. Traces of kaolin wash applied to whiten the manta remain on the piece. Manta, 57" x 81" (SAR 1981-8-1); carrying case, 35" x 25" (SAR M.524).

and white weft sets will also vary in width. The design will be built from bars and rectangles of three shades: solid black where black wefts and warps cross, solid white where white wefts and warps cross, and mixed black and white where the two elements differ. Twill patterns may coincide with color units, as when diamond figures are the same width as a black or white rectangle or stripe.

Whiting (1969:12) records a small, plain-weave plaid blanket, indifferently woven and simple in pattern, that was submitted to the 1962 Hopi Craftsman Show as part of a set of equipment used in playing a parchesi-like game. The blanket was said to have been passed from player to player along with the dice and to have been placed over a player's head when he participated in the game. The equipment also included "dice, counter, a small basket to hold the dice, [and] an extraordinary woven playing board. . . ."

Plaid patterns apparently were traditional for men's shirts as well as for blankets in the nineteenth-century Hopi towns. A handsome sleeveless shirt patterned in white and indigo blue twill, now in the National Museum of Natural History, was collected at Hopi by Major J. W. Powell in the 1870s, and a plain-weave black and white plaid shirt made at Hotevilla was submitted to the Hopi Craftsman Show in 1930 as an "old style man's shirt" (Whiting 1969–78). A small boy's plaid blanket was sometimes modified into a poncho by cutting a hole at the center for his head. Reportedly, the Hopis also used plaid fabrics as wool wraparound leggings.

It is in the twill-weave plaid fabrics and certain of the womens' mantas described in the next few pages (as, for example, the white manta with red and blue borders) that the true technical virtuosity of historic Pueblo weavers shows to best advantage. These skills can be traced directly back to the Pueblos' Anasazi forebears, who had mastered a remarkable variety of twill techniques.

Figure 37. Photographed about 1900, some of these Hopi dancers wear embroidered cotton mantas, and others, white mantas with red and blue borders. (Courtesy Natural History Museum of Los Angeles County, photo by A. C. Vroman.)

WOMEN'S MANTAS

Rectangular cotton blankets or mantas are common in archaeological sites and apparently served as clothing for both sexes. Most examples are fragmentary, but several complete blankets have been found. These are woven in striped or figured twill weave or in plain weave that might be white, painted, decorated with openwork designs, or tie-dyed. Six types of mantas, each of which has its pre-Spanish equivalent, have been made in historic times: the Hopi white cotton wedding manta, the white cotton manta with embroidered borders, the woman's white manta with indigo blue and red borders, the woman's black wool dress with indigo blue diamond twill borders, the Zuni black wool dress with blue embroidered borders, and the black wool manta with red embroidered borders. All may be worn as shoulder blankets or wraparound dresses, except possibly the Zuni type, which is said to have served only as a dress. These six manta types may represent styles that originated in different prehistoric southwestern cultures.

Hopi White Cotton Wedding Mantas. Plain-weave, white cotton mantas without decoration of any kind are found in a great many southwestern archaeological sites. It appears that every man, woman, and child had one that served as a wearing blanket or dress in life and as a burial shroud in death. Unquestionably this is a very ancient, indigenous form of textile.

Its importance is memorialized by the Hopis, who customarily present a bride with two white cotton mantas and a heavily fringed white cotton sash at one point in the wedding rituals (Nequatewa and Colton 1933). Traditionally the outfit was made for her from cotton spun and woven by the men of the groom's family. She receives it in exchange for quantities of cornmeal and other foodstuffs. One of the mantas she wears as a shoulder robe during the ceremony. The other is wrapped in the reed "suitcase" she carries, along with the sash (Fig. 35). The sash and one of the mantas are eventually buried with her at her death. Some Hopis say that after a woman's spirit is transformed into a cloud person, the loosely woven manta permits fine, gentle rain to fall to earth, while larger drops fall from the fringes of the sash (Parsons 1939: 172–73). The second manta may be embroidered after the wedding ceremonies,

Figure 38. A doll representing the Zuni Shalako kachina, a figure so tall that he must be dressed in two white cotton mantas, here painted in imitation of embroidery, with a cotton kilt around his shoulders. Height 23". (SAR C.6.)

traded to other Pueblos, or cut up and recycled into some other form. Many kilts have been cut from larger cloths, and one small manta in the School of American Research collection (T348) was embroidered on one edge, then cut up the middle and the two pieces sewn together to make a breechcloth with decorated ends.

Long, heavy, red, white, and black yarn tassels with feathers attached were fastened at the bottom corners of the Hopi wedding manta (Fig. 36), and tassels of simpler design were added at the upper corners. The tassels symbolize the bride's uterus and the feathers represent the souls of children to come and prayers for brightness and joy in life (Nequatewa and Colton 1933:Figs. 4,5). All the brides of the year, wearing their white robes, appear at the close of their village's Niman kachina ceremonies in July. Each father-in-law at this time has fastened a roll of black yarn bound with white cotton to the back of his daughter-in-law's robe between the shoulders. This is her marriage certificate. It is later removed and is not found on most wedding mantas in museum collections.

Embroidered White Cotton Mantas. Plain-weave white cotton mantas decorated with embroidery in wool along their top and bottom edges are used today as dance costumes by all the Pueblos (Figs. 37, 38). They may be worn as

Figure 39. A Hopi man with two elaborately embroidered white cotton mantas, about 1902. (Courtesy Natural History Museum of Los Angeles County, photo by A. C. Vroman.)

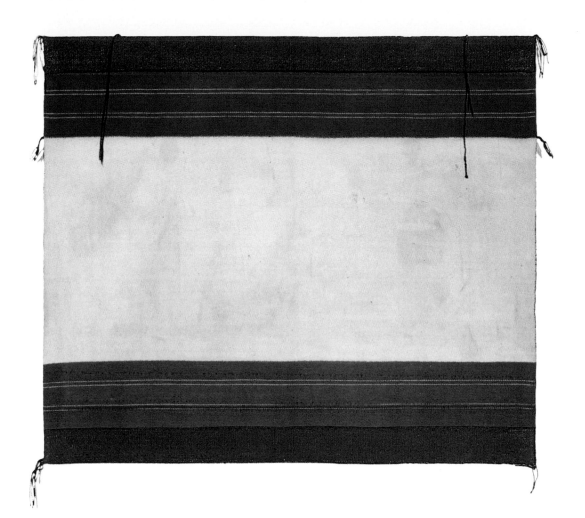

Plate 11. This plain-weave, white cotton manta, dating between 1920 and 1925, has red inner borders woven in 3/1 diagonal twill and indigo blue outer borders in four-thread diamond twill. 38" x 45". (SAR T.20.)

Plate 12. A fine example of the Zuni black wool twill-weave manta with borders embroidered in indigo blue, this piece was made between about 1870 and 1880. 40" x 50". (SAR T.38.)

dresses or shawls or, with the top folded under, as kilts by male dancers in some ceremonies.

Early classic period mantas display predominantly black embroidery with negative line designs formed by the white ground cloth, the patterns resembling those on prehistoric Pueblo III black and white pottery and textiles. The deep lower border is divided horizontally into three zones (Pl. 8). The narrow outer zone, containing a very simple design, is separated from a broad middle zone by a single line of black stitching. The third, or inner, zone contains repeats of a triangle motif—traditionally four repeats in all. Centered below each triangle motif, within the broad design zone, is a small diamond-shaped figure. In a few rare old pieces this figure contains only negative line patterns. Usually, however, a motif is worked out in colored yarns within the diamond. It may represent a butterfly, rainbow, sunflower, or some other symbol of importance in Pueblo ideology (Pl. 9). Over the years these motifs have become very elaborate, and the bright, synthetic-dyed commercial yarns used in them recently appear quite garish in contrast to the raveled reds and vegetal-dyed, handspun yellows or greens in which classic period motifs are worked.

A narrow band of embroidery embellishes the upper edge of each manta. The outer zone of the band matches that of the lower border and is separated

Figure 40. Border designs on this plain-weave white manta are loom-woven brocade; only the colored motifs are embroidered. The manta, longer than wide, was woven on a treadle loom. It was collected at Zuni, probably in the late 1930s. 46½" x 38½". (SAR T.357.)

Figure 41. A Hopi man, his legs wrapped in a traditional striped wool blanket, uses two temples as he weaves a white manta with red and blue borders, about 1882. One temple regulates the width of the upper border and the other stretches the fabric just below the work area. (Courtesy Museum of New Mexico, photo no. 16073, photo by John K. Hillers.)

from an inner zone by a single black line. The inner zone is composed of a row of triangle-and-hook motifs, obviously related to the motif common on prehistoric textiles from central Arizona.

Perhaps to relieve the monotony of the black embroidery, pairs of broad green lines, traditionally four pairs in all, cut vertically through both lower and upper border patterns. There are a few exceptionally rare and beautiful old Acoma cotton mantas embroidered in raveled red yarns (Pl. 10).

The white center portions of classic period cotton mantas usually remained undecorated, although some mantas credited to Acoma have pairs of birdlike figures centered just below their upper borders (Douglas 1937). These figures are almost identical to motifs in weft-wrap openwork on Hohokam and Mogollon cotton fabrics dating between A.D. 1100 and 1400, as are other motifs within the embroidered borders of Acoma black mantas and on white cotton shirts from Acoma and Jemez. Some cotton mantas woven at Hopi since 1900 feature elaborate, realistic representations of butterflies, birds, rainbows, and so forth embroidered on their centers between the two borders (Fig. 39).

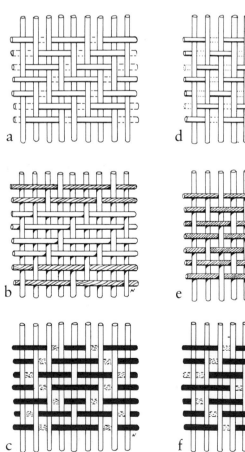
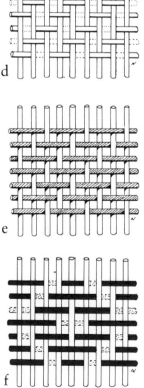

Figure 42. Twill weaves found on two white mantas with red and blue borders. The order in which heddles and shed rod are pulled to make the pattern is shown in each diagram. Left column, SAR T.427: (a) 2/2 balanced diagonal twill in the white cotton center of the manta. (b) 3/1 unbalanced diagonal twill in the red border, with white stripes in the same rhthym. (c) Three-thread diamond twill in the indigo blue border. Right column, SAR T.406: (d) 1/2 unbalanced twill in the white manta center. (e) 2/1 unbalanced twill in the red border, with white stripes. (f) Three-thread diamond twill in the indigo blue border.

A few Rio Grande women have recently created new motifs of their own. For the most part, however, embroidery on contemporary mantas replicates that found on classic pieces, the artisans often turning to Mera's (1943) illustrations for inspiration or visiting local museums to study classic pieces. Nowadays some dance mantas are decorated by appliqué designs that look from a distance like traditional embroideries. In at least one instance that I know of, the effect of embroidery was achieved by using a brocade technique on a manta woven on a treadle loom (Fig. 40).

Women's White Mantas with Blue and Red Borders. The white-centered manta with red and blue borders (Fig. 41, Pl. 11) is called the "maiden shawl" in most references because it was thought to have been worn only by young girls before marriage. In fact, women of all ages wore such shawls when they went "out walking," and the type survives as an important article of costume in many Pueblo ceremonies today. Some are woven by the Hopis, and others are made from white commercial cloth with red and blue cloth sewn on as borders. According to Titiev (1944:196), a manta of this sort was given to a Hopi girl shortly after her kachina initiation, usually between ages eight and twelve. It was made for her by her grandfather. A woman later received such a manta as one of her wedding garments. It was not to be worn during the wedding rituals but subsequently on dress and ceremonial occasions.

The white manta with red and blue borders undoubtedly finds its direct ancestor in the striped cotton twill-weave fabrics of the prehistoric Pueblos. Such pieces were patterned by black or brown, red, and white weft stripes. The dark stripes were woven either in diamond pattern or in twill diagonals that changed direction to give the dark color texture. Red and white stripes were woven in plain diagonal twill (Kent 1957:564).

Historic mantas vary in their technical details, but ordinarily the warps and center wefts are white cotton yarns, and the red and blue border wefts, wool. Before about 1850, only wool was used (Wright 1979:17). The white center is normally diagonal twill in a 2/2 rhythm but may be woven in 1/2 twill or plain weave (Fig. 42). The red inner borders are 2/1 or 3/1 diagonal twill, with the long surface floats compacted to make a dense red band. On the underside appear tiny red "stitches" one warp wide; this is the only wide-loom-woven Pueblo textile having a right and a wrong side (Fig. 43). Two, three, or more narrow white stripes cut horizontally through the red band.

Figure 43. The surface and underside of a red and blue bordered manta. The white center is woven in 1/2 diagonal twill, the red borders in 2/1 diagonal twill, and the blue borders in four-thread diamond twill. 29" x 36". (SAR T.117.)

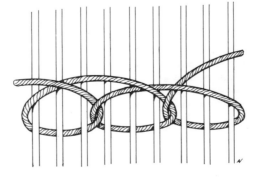

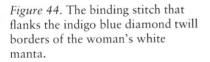

Figure 44. The binding stitch that flanks the indigo blue diamond twill borders of the woman's white manta.

The outer borders are very dark indigo blue in four-thread or three-thread diamond twill. In some shawls made since 1930, black replaces indigo. Tight binding stitches (Fig. 44) in indigo blue wool yarns flank the diamond twill borders. Since wefts in the red and blue borders are forced down tightly during weaving, the borders feel much thicker than the white center portion of the manta.

White-centered mantas worn by little girls in the late nineteenth and early twentieth centuries were often entirely of wool, indifferently woven in plain weave throughout and sometimes with natural brown outer borders instead of indigo blue. Many of these were woven not by Pueblos but by Navajos, who say that these mantas were once worn in the Yeibechai dance (Joe Ben Wheat, personal communication 1982).

One variation of this type of manta has black or blue diamond twill borders only, without the red inner border. Hopis say this is the early form made before raveled or commercial red yarns became available in quantity. A fragment of early eighteenth-century Hopi cloth torn from a white manta seems to confirm this statement: it is diagonal twill white wool with a diamond twill indigo blue border.

Classic period white-centered mantas from Laguna Pueblo stand apart in being woven entirely of very finely spun wool yarns and in having the two innermost of four red stripes broken into sets of three, rather than appearing as continuous stripes (Douglas 1939:163).

Black Wool Manta-Dresses. Until 1875 or 1880, and into the 1900s at Hopi, the everyday garb of Pueblo women included black, diagonal twill-weave wool

Figure 45. Photographed about 1900, these Hopi girls are clad in black blanket-dresses and shoulder mantas. The girl on the left wears an under-manta of commercial cloth, the second girl, one that probably is a Navajo-woven wool blanket. (Courtesy Mennonite Library and Archives, North Newton, Kansas, H. R. Voth Collection.)

mantas with indigo blue diamond twill borders (Figs. 45, 46). Women wore these as wraparound dresses held at the waist with the traditional red wool belt. The manta-dress is definitely pre-Spanish, for similar black blanket-dresses are illustrated in the Pottery Mound murals (Fig. 47). Such manta-dresses are still worn in dances and on special occasions, but with a European-style cotton dress or a commercial cloth manta underneath.

Warps and the wefts in the center portions of classic period mantas are natural brown or black wool yarns; wefts are usually tinted with native black dye to produce a more even tone. Border wefts are indigo blue. Binding stitches in indigo blue yarns flank the diamond twill borders exactly as in the diamond borders of the white cotton mantas previously described. Binding the border along its inner edge would have served to hold wefts securely in position while the piece was reversed on the loom. Some black mantas have a second "border" inside the diamond twill borders, consisting of decorative, horizontal raised lines or ridges (Fig. 48). Known to the Hopis as "hills and vales," this device was also used to decorate men's indigo blue wool shirts and breechcloths.

The black center and dark blue borders contrast little in color, and the diamond pattern tends to be lost. Women at Acoma Pueblo customarily dipped the manta in black dye when age began to dull its luster, thus blurring even more the distinction between border and center and giving the blue a brownish tinge (Douglas 1939a:156).

Among the Hopis, new black mantas served as shoulder blankets in cold weather and later were refashioned into dresses as they became worn (Wright 1979:18). Pictures of Hopi girls and women at the turn of the twentieth cen-

Figure 46. Luther Denebe of Old Oraibi, Arizona, in 1964 wove this woman's manta with diamond twill, indigo blue borders. 42" x 54". (SAR T.717.)

Figure 47. In a painted reproduction from a Pottery Mound kiva mural, a female figure wears a black manta-dress decorated with white motifs in resist-dye and holds a basket plaque similar to those still made at Hopi. (Courtesy Maxwell Museum of Anthropology, University of New Mexico.)

tury show them clad in black dresses and mantas, for which they were teased by small boys who called them crows. It has always been the custom to add green and red yarns along the inner edges of the diamond twill borders when the garment is used as a dress. These are removed when the piece is discarded. The Rio Grande Pueblos in historic times have elaborated their costume not only by wearing a variety of undergarments but also by adding a fancy apron of commercial cloth about the waist, hanging a patterned "back apron" from their shoulders, and wearing a commercial silk shawl, heavily fringed.

Since about 1900, synthetic blue dye or commercial blue yarns have replaced indigo blue handspun in the borders. While many of the black dresses worn by Pueblo dancers today are heirloom pieces, there has been an increasing use of commercially woven black wool cloth in Rio Grande Pueblo dance costumes in the last fifty years or so.

According to Spier (1924:185–86), at Zuni the twill weave center of a woman's black manta was woven with the weft carried on two separate bobbins. These he describes as "wooden rods, a quarter inch in diameter and twenty-two inches long, with a shallow groove near each end to keep the yarn from slipping off. The yarn is wound lengthwise on the bobbin, crossing from side to side, and with an extra loop around each end." In weaving, one bobbin is inserted in a shed carrying the weft from left to right. The second bobbin is inserted in the next shed and carries the weft in the same direction. These two wefts alternate throughout the cloth, both moving first from left to right, next from right to left, and so on. The normal Pueblo manner of weaving is to use a single bobbin of weft, which is carried back and forth through successive sheds.

The process described by Spier may be unique to Zuni and thus may furnish a clue for museum curators seeking to identify the source of a black

Figure 48. The corner of a black wool manta woven probably in the late 1800s shows an inner "border" of horizontal weft ridges. 36" x 40". (Laboratory of Anthropology 9079/12.)

Figure 49. One corner of a Zuni embroidered manta displays a yarn ring tassel; a tightly overcast warp selvage; two rows of chevron stitches inside the selvage; a principal design zone embroidered with swallowtail butterflies; two rows of outline stitches inside this design zone and extending up the manta edge; and a scalloped line with an asymmetric floral element worked in overcast and satin stitches. (SAR T.38.)

wool manta-dress. In the School of American Research collection there is one twill manta woven in this manner, and it is indeed from Zuni.

Navajo women, copying the style of their Pueblo teachers, wove black mantas with blue borders until 1885 or 1890. Though rarely found in museum collections, such mantas can easily be mistaken for Pueblo items. For example, the School of American Research collection includes two Navajo-made black mantas, one collected at Tesuque Pueblo and the other at the modern city of Taos, that were both originally catalogued as Pueblo. The presence of lazy lines and several other technical irregularities mark these pieces as Navajo instead.

Zuni Black Wool Mantas with Embroidered Borders. Zuni women's black wool mantas of the classic period were decorated with narrow borders of indigo blue embroidery along their upper and lower edges (Pl. 12). Some Zunis say these mantas were always used as dresses, never as shawls. Such mantas have not been made since 1875 or 1880, having been replaced by the standard, twill-weave black wool dress with indigo blue, diamond twill-weave borders.

Zuni mantas show almost no variation in materials, technical details, or designs. Warps and wefts of single-ply, handspun, natural blackish-brown wool are dyed a deep solid black with native dye. The center of the manta is 2/2 diagonal twill weave, but about four inches of plain weave appear along the warp edges. Embroidery is carried out over the plain weave and in very narrow lines up the weft edges, with identical designs on the two borders. Selvages are composed of three two-ply black or indigo blue yarns. Warp selvages are tightly overcast, or whipped, with single-ply, handspun indigo blue yarns. Corner tassels, tied to the manta by the ends of the selvage yarns, are either yarn rings or small bundles of brownish-black yarn (Fig. 49).

Strict conventions governed the five types of stitches used in various parts of the embroidery, all carried out with paired indigo blue yarns. On any museum piece, one finds two rows of herringbone stitches just inside the whipped warp selvages (Fig. 50). Inside these is the main design panel, worked in the traditional Pueblo stitch but with the paired yarns not twisted between stitches. Along the inner edge of the panel is a double row of outline stitches, and inside this a scalloped line of embroidery made by overcasting stitches or satin stitches that parallel the warps. Extending from the scalloped line at intervals is a floral motif also worked in overcast stitch. Each motif appears to repre-

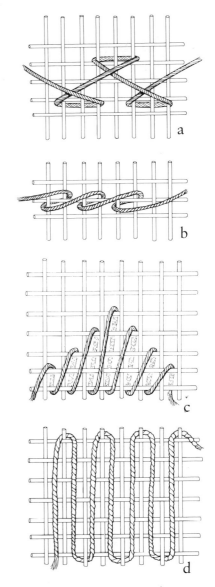

Figure 50. Four embroidery stitches that are sometimes used in conjunction with the regular Pueblo stitch: (a) herringbone stitch; (b) outline stitch; (c) overcast stitch; (d) satin stitch.

Figure 51. Three common negative-line designs from the borders of Zuni black wool mantas: the swallowtail butterfly, an hourglass figure, and diamond figures. (Drawing by Julie Wagner.)

Figure 52. This black wool manta embroidered in raveled red yarns and indigo blue handspun wool was made at Acoma Pueblo between about 1850 and 1860. 48" x 54". (SAR T.468.)

sent a single, asymmetric blossom set at an angle to warp and weft. Up each weft edge of the manta runs a double row of outline stitches with small triangles or flowers spaced along it.

I have seen only five motifs apart from the flower, which is a Spanish acquisition. All are geometric in form. Three of the most common are a swallowtail butterfly, an hour glass, and a diamond (Fig. 51). The swallowtail butterfly, a woman's symbol and a symbol of beauty in Zuni ideology (B. Tedlock, personal communication, 1981), is often the only motif on a border, the butterflies being placed with their heads alternately up and down. Although they are shown as black figures in the drawings, the motifs are actually negative line designs, formed by the small areas of black ground cloth showing between the dark indigo blue stitches. The contrast between dark blue and black is so subtle that design details are not easily seen, and it is not surprising that Mera (1943:71) failed to include heads on his drawings of butterflies.

Embroidered Black Wool Mantas. Until the end of the classic period, Acoma craftsmen wove black wool mantas with borders lavishly embroidered in red with touches of indigo blue (Fig. 52, Plates 13 and 14). In the twentieth century, the art was revived using commercial materials. Some of the Tewas claim they also embroidered black wool mantas (Pl. 15), and a few, quite simple in design, were also produced at Zuni. Embroidery on the Zuni pieces is done with paired, untwisted yarns as on Zuni indigo blue embroidered mantas.

Red embroidery yarns in the fine old Acoma mantas were raveled from Spanish or Anglo-American commercial cloth containing presynthetic dyes. Tests on six mantas at the Denver Art Museum and two (T.44 and T.468) at the School of American Research show the red to be lac or cochineal. All other yarns were of handspun wool dyed with indigo or native black or green. Unlike the rigidly conventional Zuni mantas, these pieces vary greatly in weav-

Plate 13. Embroidery designs on Acoma mantas combine the Spanish floral motif with prehistoric design elements from the Anasazi (negative patterning and terraced triangles), Sinagua-Salado (triangle-and-hook), and Hohokam (diamond-shaped units). This piece dates between 1850 and 1860. 48" x 57". (SAR T.699.)

Plate 14. Probably woven as a plain black manta between 1850 and 1860, this Acoma piece has diamond twill, indigo blue borders beneath the embroidery. The curving leaf pattern and small crosses are unusual for Pueblo work. 46" x 55". (SAR T.122.)

Plate 15. The embroidered borders of four black wool mantas are compared here. From top to bottom: SAR T.44, possibly Tesuque, 1850–60, 59" wide; SAR T.356, San Juan, 1941, probably woven originally as a dress; SAR T.437, Zuni, 1875–80; SAR T.468, Acoma, 1850–60.

Plate 16. This handsomely embroidered shirt, made entirely of commercial materials, was purchased from Frank Toledo of Jemez Pueblo in 1927. Body 46" x 23". (SAR T.12.)

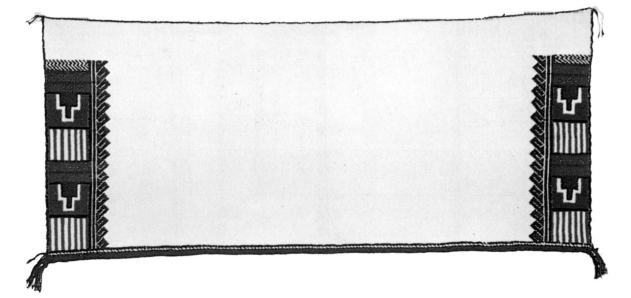

Plate 17. Though made in 1964, this kilt follows closely the traditional design with triangle-and-hook motif and black braid sewn to the lower border. It was handwoven from commercial cotton string and yarns by Luther Denebe of Old Oraibi. 57" x 24". (SAR T.716.)

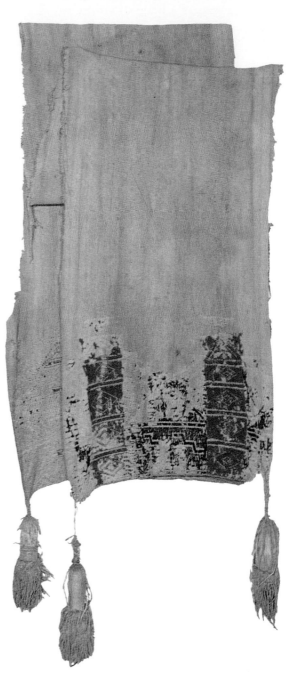

Plate 18. One end of an embroidered cotton breechcloth from Acoma, 1800–1850, shows negative line patterning, terraced triangles, and small squares with center dots that are reminiscent of prehistoric Anasazi textile designs. 20½" x 16½". (SAR T.93.)

Plate 19. A type of cotton garment not made by the Pueblos since the late 1800s, this Jemez breechcloth could easily date between 1800 and 1850. The red yarns were raveled from lac-dyed commercial cloth. 84" x 17". (SAR T.395.)

ing and embroidery techniques and design motifs. Two stitches not found on other embroideries—a countered outline stitch and a chain stitch (Fig. 53)—are used to define pattern zones.

The top and bottom borders of the Acoma mantas are identical in design, each about twelve inches deep, with the field divided horizontally into three zones: a broad outer one, a narrow middle zone, and a third zone consisting of repeats of a floral motif along the inner edge of the border. The designs of the outer and middle zones bear no apparent relationship to one another. Within the red portions of the pattern, design motifs may appear as negative lines of black ground cloth or may be worked in indigo blue yarns. Motifs within the indigo blue sections are black negative line designs that are very difficult to see (Fig. 54). The Acoma flower seen on these pieces, unlike the Zuni flower, is bilaterally symmetrical, composed of two equal parts that appear to represent two blossoms. As with Acoma embroideries on cotton, several of the geometric motifs originated in prehistoric weft-wrap openwork designs.

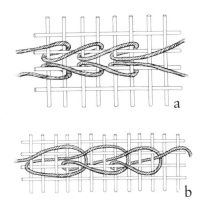

Figure 53. Two stitches found in Acoma embroidery: (a) countered outline stitch; (b) chain stitch.

MEN'S SHIRTS

Patterned after prehistoric Pueblo cotton shirts (Kent 1957:607–609), traditional Pueblo and Navajo men's shirts were constructed from three separately woven cloths of wool or cotton: a large rectangle with a center hole for the head, and two sleeves (Fig. 55). By progressively tightening the weave, each sleeve was shaped on the loom to be wide at the shoulder and narrow at the cuff. Sleeves were sewn on at the shoulder and sewn or tied shut at the cuff. The front and back of the shirt were not seamed together but were held loosely by ties.

Wool shirts were generally of twill weave in dark indigo blue or black, sometimes with horizontal red stripes. Some, lacking sleeves, were simply worn like small ponchos (see Fig. 62). Hopi shirts of the mid-1800s were apparently plaid-patterned.

Since the 1920s, craftsmen at Jemez Pueblo have specialized in embroidered white shirts made of commercial cotton cloth (Pl. 16), a type of garment once hand-woven and embroidered at Acoma and perhaps other Pueblos

Figure 54. The surface and underside of a black wool manta show black negative patterning against red (light) and indigo blue (dark) embroidery. Small, random stitches appear on the underside of Pueblo embroidery in contrast to the regular rows of yarns on the underside of brocade pieces. Notice the unusual diamond twill weave of the manta center. 42" x 59". (SAR T.44.)

Figure 55. Woven from handspun, synthetic-dyed black wool in 2/2 twill, this traditional Pueblo shirt was made at Hopi in 1928. Body 23" long, 21" wide. (SAR T.22.)

Figure 56. A prehistoric openwork shirt made by interlinking cotton yarns, from Tonto National Monument, about 1300. Length 26". (Courtesy Arizona State Museum, The University of Arizona, photo by E. B. Sayles.)

(Douglas 1939c). These shirts are the historic version of a white cotton shirt with a painted design from Poncho House (A.D. 1100–1300) in northern Arizona. Embroidered vests are a recent phenomenon, a modification of the traditional shirt made for use in dance costumes or for tourist sale.

Prehistorically the Pueblos used finger techniques to produce white, openwork cotton shirts, examples of which come from Tonto National Monument (Fig. 56), and from White House Ruin (A.D. 1100–1300) in Canyon de Chelly, Arizona. Under the influence of the Spaniards, the Pueblo people substituted the techniques of knitting with needles and crocheting for the old openwork methods. Crocheted cotton dance shirts are presently made at San Juan Pueblo, and white, commercial cloth dance shirts with panels of crochet and embroidery set in at yoke and sleeve are a product of Isleta Pueblo (see Fig. 77). Sandia Pueblo men formerly wore cotton shirts decorated with drawn work (Douglas 1939c:164); today, lace is used. Lace, drawn work, and embroidered or crocheted panels probably replaced the decoration in gauze weave and weft-wrap openwork common in prehistoric textiles.

KILTS

Male dancers in many Pueblo ceremonies wear white cotton kilts (Fig. 57). Wrapped around the hips, these rectangular cloths cover each dancer from waist to knee, the embroidered ends meeting along the right thigh or some-

Figure 57. Hopi dancers wearing white kilts with embroidered borders, about 1905. (Courtesy John P. Wilson, photo by Joseph Mora.)

Figure 58. Three kilt ends embroidered in green, red, and black. The terraced triangles are said to represent clouds, the vertical red lines, rain. All three kilts have the traditional black braid sewn to the bottom edge with slanted stitches, representing falling rain. Only the center kilt has small black rectangles embroidered above the braid. (Left to right: SAR 1978-4-86, 43" x 24", 1950–60; SAR M.539, 1950–60; SAR T.491, 1910–30.)

times at the back. Kilts may also be fastened to a long pole and carried as a banner in some ceremonies.

The embroidered kilt design has become quite standardized since the late nineteenth century (Fig. 58, Pl. 17). It consists of a broad outer zone with motifs worked in black, red, and green. This zone is separated from a narrow inner one by a single black line. The inner zone traditionally contains a row of triangle-and-hook repeats, but these have been reduced to simple triangles on some contemporary kilts. The design in the main, or outer, zone comprises terraced triangle motifs that are said to represent clouds, along with stripes representing rain. As in cotton manta patterns, pairs of broad green lines cut vertically through the border panels, although there are only two pairs of lines on the kilt borders. Traditionally, small embroidered rectangles— usually four pairs in all—are spaced along the bottom edge, and a narrow black braid is sewn on with slanting black stitches. The black stitching and braid are said to represent rain, and the white kilt, a cloud. Sometimes designs were painted on white cotton kilts to be used in certain ceremonies (Fig. 59).

Today the Hopis weave kilts from commercial cotton and embroider them with the traditional design. Most of the kilts worn by Rio Grande Pueblo dancers are made from commercial cotton cloth, but the embroidered decoration remains as it has been since the late 1800s.

Black or dark indigo blue wool kilts are worn in some Pueblo dances. While those made at Zuni in the nineteenth century are said to have been embroidered in indigo blue with patterns like the ones on black dresses, black kilts from other pueblos are not embroidered. At present, the black "kilts" seen on many Pueblo dancers are actually black mantas folded into the kilt shape (Fig. 60).

Kilts have not been positively identified in prehistoric Anasazi Pueblo textile collections, but they are found in Hohokam and Sinagua burials and are pictured on dancers in late prehistoric Pueblo murals (Fig. 61). Kilts shown in murals at Kuaua are plain black, whereas those seen at Awatovi and Pot-

Figure 59. Dating to about 1940, this dance kilt is made of cotton sacking painted yellow, with plumed serpents, two hands, stars, and crosses painted in dark green and blue. Along the bottom edge is a band of cotton cloth painted green, from which hangs a row of tin tinklers. 40" x 18". (SAR T.376.)

tery Mound seem to show embroidery, painting, openwork, and other forms of decoration. Embroidered patterns appear along the lower borders of the kilts rather than on the ends.

BREECHCLOTHS

Historically, breechcloths were woven in white cotton or black or dark blue wool. Only six embroidered cotton breechcloths are on record, all probably made before 1875; two of them are in the School of American Research collection (Plates 18 and 19). Reconstructions of the designs on the six pieces can be found in Mera (1943:Pl. X). Coming from San Felipe, Acoma, and Jemez pueblos, the breechcloths are very long and wide (seventy to eighty inches by sixteen to eighteen inches), resembling in shape pieces from archaeological sites in central and southern Arizona. Both ends are covered with rich embroidery similar to that found on cotton mantas. Cotton breechcloth ends were decorated by appliqué at Zuni in the early 1900s and probably well before that time.

Black or indigo blue wool breechcloths were once woven in many pueblos and are worn in some ceremonies today (Fig. 62). Douglas (1940b:179) briefly described them as about forty by sixteen inches in size, with ends decorated in diamond twill in blue or black, by pairs of red stripes, or, at Zuni, by dark blue embroidery. These garments may be seen on some Hopi kachina dolls. Some black breechcloths had red and green cords near their ends attached in the same manner as the cords on women's black manta-dresses.

Breechcloths were standard, everyday clothing for Pueblo men in prehistoric and early historic times. The commercial cotton pants first made by the

Figure 60. In a portion of a 1918 painting by the San Ildefonso artist, Crescencio Martínez, a deer dancer wears a black dress folded into a kilt, a braided cotton sash, openwork leggings, and a commercial cloth shirt cut in a traditional pattern of Euro-American origin. (SAR P.20, photo by Martin Etter.)

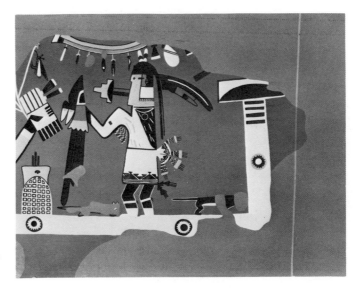

Figure 61. An Awatovi kiva mural shows a figure costumed in a white kilt with embroidered(?) border, a sash with very elaborate end tassels, and a short shoulder manta with resist-dye design. (Courtesy Peabody Museum, Harvard University, photo by Fogg Museum.)

Pueblos resembled chaps, with the two halves sewn together at the waist. The crotch, left unstitched, was covered by a breechcloth. Cotton pants worn in more recent times were constructed with a gusset so that the breechcloth was not needed. I have no information about when this modification was made; the early form was still in use at Zuni in 1879 (Stevenson n.d.:129–30) and apparently at Hopi until about 1900.

SASHES WITH ENDS PATTERNED BY "HOPI BROCADE"

Since the classic period, the Pueblos have made dance sashes with ends elaborately patterned by a technique called "Hopi brocade" (Fig. 63, Pl. 20). The earliest documented example was acquired from the Hopis by James Stevenson in 1879. The origin of the technique remains something of a mystery. No prehistoric or early historic Pueblo fabrics display such decoration, but neither is the method exactly like any European or American technique that could have been introduced in historic times. It does, however, resemble the European wrap-weave called *soumak* (Emery 1966:220).

Douglas (1938) first described the Hopi-brocade process in detail and gave it its name. It is not a true brocade, although as in brocade the colored wefts are inserted and floated over groups of warps to make a design, while a thin white weft (the tabby) alternates with them, interlacing with warps to make a plain-weave structure (Fig. 64). Unlike the wefts in standard brocade, the design wefts pass regularly over eight warps and then wrap back around the last pair of the eight. Warp pairs are controlled by a supplementary heddle.

Figure 62. In a 1970 Corn or Tablita Dance at San Ildefonso Pueblo, the two leaders wear long black breechcloths and traditional, sleeveless, poncho-like black shirts. An embroidered banner is held over the dancers' heads. (Courtesy Arizona State Museum, The University of Arizona, photo by Helga Teiwes.)

It is a curious process and may be a Pueblo invention, perhaps their adaptation of back-stitch embroidery to the loom.

The earlier sashes were woven of handspun wool, with a fine linen or cotton string tabby. More recent examples have cotton string warps, handspun or commercial wool wefts in the plain-weave portions, a fine cotton tabby, and commercial wool brocade yarns. Within the last few years, Hopi weavers have begun to substitute acrylic for wool yarns.

Sashes are woven on a narrow upright loom (Fig. 65). Two identical pieces are made, each a fairly standard forty-five inches long and ten inches wide, with brocading and fringe only on the bottom end. When finished, their undecorated upper ends are loosely lashed together to make a long sash, which is worn by male dancers in most ceremonies with the decorated ends hanging almost to the ground on the right side (Fig. 66). Occasionally a dancer wears a sash about his neck with the ends crossed over his chest, and in some dances these sashes serve as breechcloths with their brocaded ends hanging at the dancer's front and back, presumably replacing the nineteenth-century embroidered cotton breechcloth.

Figure 63. A Hopi brocaded dance sash made in 1960 illustrates the joining of two separately woven pieces and the regular vertical lines produced on the undersurface by the brocade technique. 108" x 12". (SAR 1981-2-5.)

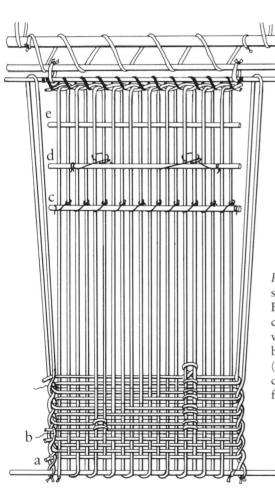

Figure 64. Diagram of the Hopi brocade technique. For the sake of clarity, the number of warps has been limited. (a) Brocade weft of colored wool. (b) Tabby of very fine linen or cotton thread that interlaces with warps in regular plain weave; in most sashes, the tabby is inserted after each brocade weft rather than after every two wefts as shown here. (c) Heddle for regular plain weave. (d) Supplementary heddle controlling pairs of warps that will be wrapped. (e) Shed rod for plain weave. (After Douglas 1938:Fig. 1.)

The sash design is standardized except in the narrow band of brocade that separates the decorated area from the plain weave. For this band, each weaver chooses his own motifs, which are often called his "signature." A strip of red cloth is customarily sewn at the end of the sash between the brocaded portion and the fringe, which is formed by twisting the unwoven warp ends together.

Normally identical in both motifs and color distribution, the design fields of most sash ends between the signature band and the red cloth strip are divided horizontally into five zones. Sharp white triangles grouped into zigzag lines form a negative pattern within the black brocade of the top and bottom zones. Inside these are bands containing three narrow stripes: a green stripe, a narrow black stripe with four or more pairs of vertical white lines incorporated in its length, and a narrow indigo blue (nowadays synthetic purple) stripe. The wide, green center band is decorated by two red, lozenge-shaped motifs that alternate with pairs of elongated, C-shaped elements placed back to back. Whiting (1977:416–l8) discusses the possible evolution of the design.

We have no information from Zuni or the Rio Grande Pueblos about the possible symbolism of this design, and there is little agreement on its meaning among weavers of the three Hopi mesas. Wright (1976:35) summarizes

Figure 65. A Hopi man weaving a dance sash, about 1898. (Courtesy Califonia Historical Society/Title Insurance and Trust Company [Los Angeles] Collection of Historical Photographs, photo by George Wharton James.)

Plate 20. Of four "Hopi-brocaded" sash ends, the two in the center (SAR T.700 and T.712) are nineteenth-century pieces, and the two at either end (SAR T.644 and T.402) were woven between 1930 and 1950. The design has remained essentially unchanged since the mid-1800s. Each piece is about 10" wide.

Plate 21. Four warp-faced belts illustrate the Navajo and Hopi traditional styles. From left to right: SAR T.86, Zuni, Navajo style, late 1800s, 108" long; SAR T.87, Zuni, Hopi style, 1920s; SAR T.701, Hopi, Navajo style, 1960s; SAR T.711, San Ildefonso, modified Hopi style, 1965.

Plate 22. These contemporary Pueblo pieces are, from left to right, a Hopi-style belt from Jemez Pueblo, 1967 (SAR T.724); a Cochiti hair tie, 1960 (SAR T.502); a pair of garters from Zuni, 1929 (SAR T.41); a San Juan belt, 1920s (SAR T.98); and a belt of unknown origin, 1947 (SAR 1981-20-1).

21   22

Plate 23. A Euro-American-style shirt with an overshirt has decoration in openwork fabric of commercial manufacture. The piece was purchased at Isleta Pueblo in 1972. Length 33". (SAR M.646.)

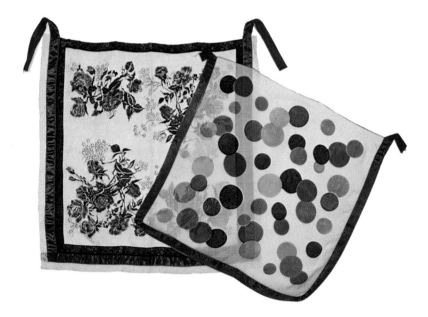

Plate 24. Of two back aprons, the one on the left is a rayon scarf with satin ribbon, from Cochiti, 1950s (SAR T.500). On the right is a China silk scarf from Japan, 32" square, purchased at Cochiti in 1964 (SAR M.581).

the interpretations gathered by Stephen in 1893 and Voth a few years later. The design, according to Stephen, represents the mask of the Broadface kachina, the white zigzag lines being his teeth, the red lozenges, his eyes, and the short paired vertical lines, face markings. Voth's informants indicated that the zigzag lines were mountain lion teeth and the lozenges, blossoms of melons, squashes, and flowers. The C-shaped lines represent the cotyledons of sprouting beans. Wade and Evans (1973) and Sayers (1981) give additional interpretations. It is probable that the original symbolic meaning, if one ever existed, has been lost to contemporary weavers, as has the symbolism of embroidery motifs. Any meaning can be attached to these designs by individual artisans, so interpretations will vary widely.

In the 1930s and early 1940s, Hopi weavers applied the brocade pattern to table runners and other articles made for sale, but they no longer do so. They do, however, make brocaded shirts and vests for use as dance costumes or for sale. Since about 1954, very narrow belts with brocaded ends have been made at Hopi as tourist novelties.

In recent years, commercial white cotton cloth dance sashes with ends embroidered in the classic brocade pattern have been produced at Jemez Pueblo. Two white commercial cloth dance sashes with embroidered ends were sold at the Santa Fe Indian Market in 1982; they were similar in size and design to the nineteenth-century breechcloths.

Figure 66. These Hopi dancers of the early 1900s wear sashes decorated by Hopi brocade. (Courtesy Natural History Museum of Los Angeles County, photo by A. C. Vroman.)

The Hopis call the wide, braided cotton sash with its long, heavy fringe the "big sash" (Fig. 67). It may also be referred to as the wedding sash, because it is one of the articles traditionally presented to a Hopi bride at her wedding, or it may be called the rain sash, for the fringe symbolizes falling rain. Its use is not limited to the Hopis; male dancers in many of the pueblos wear these sashes wrapped about the waist with the fringe usually falling on the right thigh (Fig. 68).

The big sash, in its classic form, is made by a process called *sprang* (Collingwood 1974). In this method, the yarn is wound continuously around two poles, and each interlacing movement carried out at one pole repeats itself the full length of the yarn set. The process is explained in Figures 69 and 70. Nowadays, commercial cotton string has replaced the traditional two-ply,

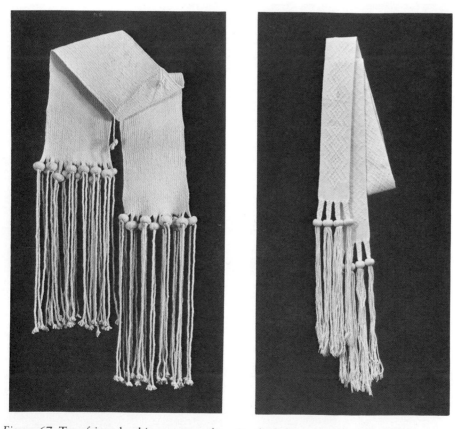

Figure 67. Two fringed, white cotton sashes. On the left is a traditional braided Hopi sash with heavy fringes falling from corn husk rings. The sash at the right, a modern version of the traditional form made at Tesuque Pueblo in 1961, is woven from white cotton string and patterned by warp floats. (Left: 92" x 8", SAR T.708, about 1930; right: 87" x 3", SAR T.589.)

handspun cotton, and white sashes are sometimes woven in twill weave or warp-float pattern weave to simulate braiding.

Handsome sashes braided in yarns spun from dog hair come from Basket-maker sites (A.D. 600) in the Four Corners region (Morris 1959), and white cotton braids are found in most later prehistoric sites (A.D. 1000–1400). A cotton braid fragment with end rings and fringing like those of the contemporary sashes was found in Tularosa Cave (about A.D. 1200) in southwestern New Mexico (Kent 1983). Unquestionably the fringed sash is a very ancient form of southwestern textile, though we have no solid evidence as to when the sprang process replaced interlacing with free-hanging yarns (see Kent 1983).

LEGGINGS

In the prehistoric Southwest, socks, leggings, shirts, and bags were fashioned by looping or interlinking (Fig. 71)—techniques that were replaced by knitting with needles and crocheting in historic times. During the seventeenth century, the Pueblos were expected to supply knitted socks to the Spanish governor in Santa Fe for distribution to the settlers. In 1640, for example, he received 1,399 pairs, and some 600 pairs were traded south to New Spain in 1659 and 1660 (Museum of International Folk Art 1979:11).

A fragment of knitted wool was found in a prehistoric Frijoles Canyon,

Figure 68. In an early twentieth-century photograph taken in a Hopi village, the dancers' white braided sashes dominate their costumes. It is easy to see why the sash fringes are said to symbolize falling rain. (Courtesy Natural History Museum of Los Angeles County, photo by A. C. Vroman.)

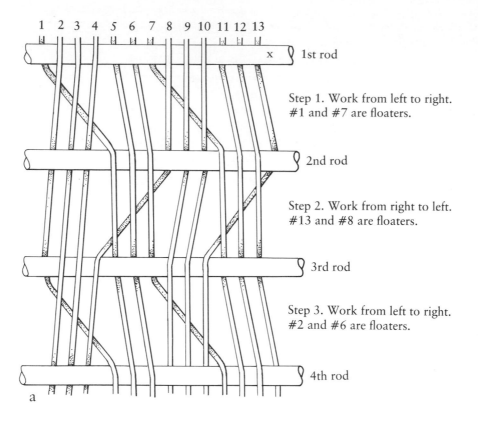

1 2 3 4 5 6 7 8 9 10 11 12 13

x   1st rod

Step 1. Work from left to right.
#1 and #7 are floaters.

2nd rod

Step 2. Work from right to left.
#13 and #8 are floaters.

3rd rod

Step 3. Work from left to right.
#2 and #6 are floaters.

4th rod

a

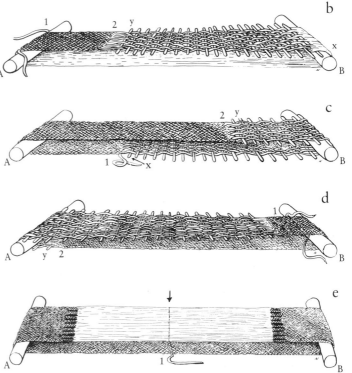

Figure 69. Diagram of the sprang technique used in braiding fringed cotton sashes. (a) Braid movements with the number of yarns reduced to thirteen (braiding can be done with any multiple of six and one extra floater yarn). (b) Worker braids from 1 to 2, inserting a rod after each step. These are pushed toward pole B. The first rod inserted is "x," the last, "y." Note that braiding is done entirely on the upper plane. (c) Sash has been slipped towards worker at pole A so that point 1, which was on the upper plane, is now in the lower plane. Retaining rod x has been slipped around pole B to a position on lower plane adjacent to point 1. (d) When braiding has continued until no more retaining rods can be inserted, point 1 is slipped on around until it is again in the upper plane near pole B. Then, beginning with x, retaining rods are removed, one by one, which automatically braids against point 1. Rod y is not removed and becomes rod x when braiding resumes at point 2 (which will be slipped around pole A to the upper plane). (e) Sash after completion of braid and small fringe braids, which contain twelve strands each, except for one composed of thirteen strands. Arrow marks point where unbraided yarns that are to form fringe will be cut so that sash may be removed from frame.

New Mexico, site that had been reoccupied by Pueblos fleeing Spanish reprisals after the 1680 rebellion, and several knitted wool sock fragments of Hopi manufacture date to the early eighteenth century. These pieces are socks with feet, rather than the footless leggings of the nineteenth and twentieth centuries. Only the Zunis have made footed socks in recent historic times.

Knit leggings appear in light and dark versions, both wool (Fig. 72). Dark leggings were traditionally indigo blue, but black is often used today. Long, white, cotton openwork leggings with a fringe down the outside of the leg are still made at San Juan (see Fig. 60); they may be a traditional Tewa style. In any event, they appear to be patterned after Plains Indian fringed skin leggings. They are usually worked in crochet, though some are knitted.

WARP-FACED BELTS AND TIES

There are two traditional styles of warp-faced belts, both with center panels patterned in warp-float (Fig. 73, Pl. 21). Both Pueblos and Navajos make and wear the so-called Navajo-style belt of red and green wool warps with

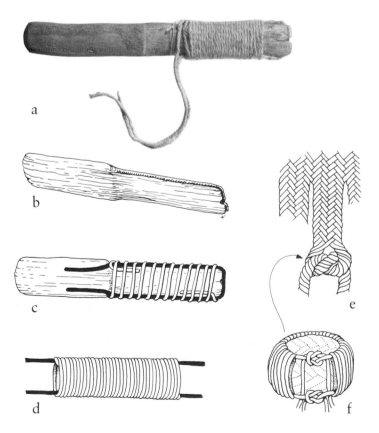

Figure 70. Method of making rings for the fringed sash. (a) Wooden tool for wrapping cotton yarns to cover braided corn husk ring. Length about 5½". (Courtesy Department of Anthropology, Smithsonian Institution.) (b) Wrapping tool, showing handle and working end with grooved edges and end notch. (c) Heavy yarn is placed in edge groove, and thinner cotton yarn is wrapped around tool over this. (d) The heavy cord has been cut through at the notch in the tool end, and the wrapping slipped off the tool. (e) A small end fringe with unbraided yarns twisted and tied into a knot, over which the wrapped corn husk ring will be slipped. (f) The cotton wrapping is drawn around a braided corn husk ring and tied in position by the heavy edge cords.

white cotton warps and wefts. These belts are also made for tourist sale. Hopi-style belts woven from red, black, and green wool warps and black cotton wefts are less common. Produced at Hopi and possibly at other pueblos, they apparently are not made or worn by Navajo women. The two types differ in design and processes of manufacture (MacLeish 1940).

Since a warp-faced fabric is one in which only the warps show, patterns can be made by floating the warps—that is, allowing them to run free on the surface of the fabric rather than interlacing them regularly with wefts. In both types of traditional Pueblo belts, the center design panel contains twice as many warps, very closely packed, as do the two outer warp-faced panels. In the Hopi-style belt, the center panel is woven from alternating black and red warps. A string-loop heddle controls (brings forward) the red warps, and a shed rod controls the black. The center panel design is built of small triangles of floated warps, a pattern created by manipulating both red and black warps with the fingers. Two design motifs, each bilaterally symmetrical, usually alternate over the length of the belt, with no background space between them.

In Navajo-style belts, the floated design in red and white is fashioned with the aid of two small supplementary heddles. Controlling alternate reds in the center panel only, these heddles serve to create long red floats on the belt's surface (Fig. 74). Again, two motifs alternate along the belt, but usually with unpatterned spaces between them. Motifs are made up of various combinations of small triangles and vertical and horizontal lines. They are more

Figure 71. This prehistoric Pueblo shoe-sock comes from Nitsi Canyon, northern Arizona, about 1200. The sole is of yucca fiber, the sock portion of cotton and wool pile cord in a loop technique. Length of sole 11½". (Courtesy Arizona State Museum, The University of Arizona, photo by E. B. Sayles.)

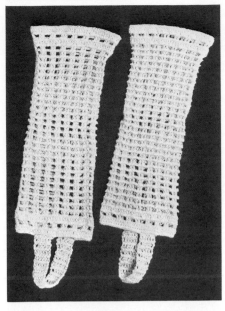

a

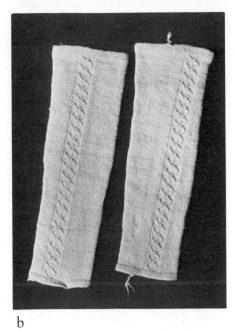

b

c

d

Figure 72. A variety of Pueblo leggings. (a) A pair crocheted by Romalda Lujan, Isleta Pueblo, 1972 (14" long, SAR M.647). (b) Handspun wool leggings knit by Luke Kewanousi, Hopi, 1945–55 (SAR T.497). (c) A knit pair with fringe attached, from San Juan Pueblo, 1940 (SAR T.503). (d) Commercial wool leggings knit by Caroline Pecos, Cochiti Pueblo, 1975 (SAR 1981-2-4).

varied and complicated than those on Hopi-style belts, but neither sort of design has any known symbolism today.

Garters are woven in exactly the same manner as Navajo-style belts but are smaller and more simply patterned. Hair ties, though warp-faced, do not contain warp-float patterns (Pl. 22).

Warp-faced tie and belt fragments patterned by warp-float designs similar to those on historic pieces have been found at the Salado ruins in Tonto National Monument but not in Anasazi sites. The technique, however, was apparently introduced to the Pueblos before the arrival of the Spaniards, as evidenced by one figure in the Awatovi murals that appears to be wearing a warp-faced belt. I know of one early eighteenth-century Pueblo belt that was woven in exactly the same technique as the twentieth-century, Navajo-style Zuni belt (T.86) illustrated in Figure 73, indicating that this technique was known to the Pueblos in very early Spanish times. It was probably taught to Navajo women along with blanket weaving in the l600s.

The weaving of warp-patterned belts is currently an important art among traditional weavers from northern Arizona and New Mexico south through

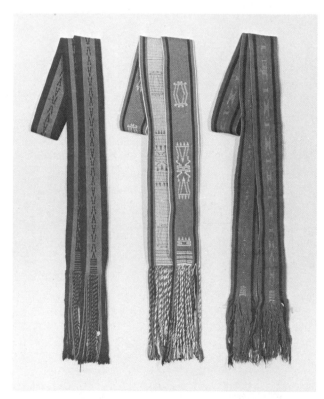

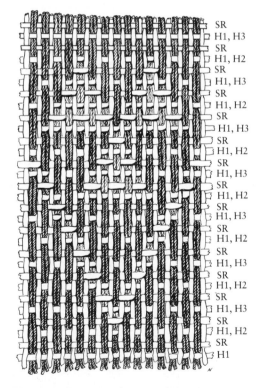

Figure 73. Three warp-float belts. Left: Navajo-style belt, Hopi, 1960s (106" x 4", SAR T.701). Center: Navajo-style belt collected at Zuni in 1929, woven as shown in Figure 74; unlike most belts of this type, one motif repeats itself the length of the belt with no space between motifs (SAR T.86). Right: Hopi-style belt, Santo Domingo, 1960s (SAR T.689).

Figure 74. Diagram showing the order in which heddles are pulled in weaving the warp-float center of a Navajo-style belt. Heddle 1 brings forward all white warps, shed rod all colored warps. Heddle 2 brings forward all odd-numbered colored warps, and heddle 3 all even-numbered colored warps. Heddles 2 and 3 are pulled alternately with heddle 1, thus floating colored warps to make a design that shows on one surface and appears in white on the underside.

Mexico, Central America, and western South America to southern Chile. Usable, easily packed, and relatively inexpensive, belts are an ideal sales item for tourists, a fact that explains their increased production in recent times. Since the 1920s, Pueblo weavers have used a variety of nontraditional colors and designs in their warp-patterned belts.

RABBIT-FUR BLANKETS

Warm blankets of rabbit-fur yarn (Fig. 75) were once made by native peoples from the Yucatan northward up the west coast of Mexico and throughout North America west of the Rocky Mountains to the Arctic Circle. Found archaeologically in Great Basin sites dated to roughly 8000 B.C., fur cord very early answered the need for warm clothing and offered a practical alternative to the skins of harder-to-procure large animals such as bear and buffalo. Rabbit-fur robes sized to fit the individual man, woman, child, or tiny infant made up part of the burial wrappings in almost every Anasazi Basketmaker site (A.D. 200–600) in northeastern Arizona.

The prehistoric Pueblos later substituted feather cord for fur cord, but in historic times fur cord again came into vogue, at least among the Hopis. There is little information about its use by historic Rio Grande peoples, although

Figure 75. A nineteenth-century rabbit-fur blanket from Hopi. (Courtesy Peabody Museum, Harvard University, photo by Hillel Berger.)

Figure 76. A Hopi Ogre kachina in a rabbit-fur blanket, about 1902. (Courtesy Mennonite Library and Archives, North Newton, Kansas, H. R. Voth Collection.)

fur robes are said to have been present in San Juan Pueblo until about 1900 (Fox 1978:67). One Hopi kachina *(Chavaiyo)* of Eastern Pueblo derivation wears a rabbit-fur robe, indicating that the garment was traditional at one time in the New Mexico villages (Stephen 1936:175). Fur robes were very much in evidence among the Hopis in the late nineteenth century, serving as kachina costumes (Fig. 76), shoulder robes, bedding, and burial shrouds (Stephen 1936).

There were many technical variations in the way fur cord was made and fur blankets woven. Usually, however, cordage was fashioned by wrapping long strips of rabbit fur, softened in water, around a coarse cord. As the strip dried, it shrank and held fast to the cord. Strips of fur cord, placed as close together as possible, functioned as warps and were held in position by twining pairs of wefts between them at intervals of two inches or so. According to Stephen (1936:274), Hopis strung the fur cord strips along a heavy cord and then twined wefts through these free-hanging warps. In prehistoric examples the wefts and the cores of the warps are yucca-fiber yarn, but as soon as wool became available in the 1600s, it replaced yucca.

Traditionally, rabbit-fur robes were made by women, five or six of them working together on a single piece. Fur robes were discarded in the early twentieth century in favor of commercial wool blankets, which were easier to get and to keep free of moths and other vermin. By 1930 only four elderly Hopi women retained the art of fur robe making. They produced six robes between

Figure 77. Made by Demacia Lucero Cariz of Isleta Pueblo, this modern shirt has decorative panels in an openwork commercial fabric. It is embroidered with a prehistoric Hohokam motif in double running stitch. Length 43". (SAR 1981-5.)

1930 and 1945. Subsequently, from 1951 to 1966, two men at Oraibi and Hotevilla wove rabbit-fur blankets, but on their regular upright looms, using wool warps and fur cord wefts woven in and tamped down with a batten, as in cloth weaving. These blankets were sold to museums and collectors (Whiting 1970). Rabbit-fur blankets recently woven at Taos Pueblo on treadle looms bear even less resemblance to the traditional article. The warps are wool, and wool wefts alternate with strips of rabbit fur.

EUROPEAN-PUEBLO TRADITIONAL STYLES

Today, the everyday dress of Pueblo Indians is essentially identical to that of other American people. However, certain Euro-American-derived elements of costume have become traditional for wear on special occasions and as parts of dance costumes. Some of these stem from Spanish styles, their acceptance by the Pueblos as traditional articles becoming firmly established after 1846 in reaction to new styles being introduced by Anglo-Americans. This Spanish-

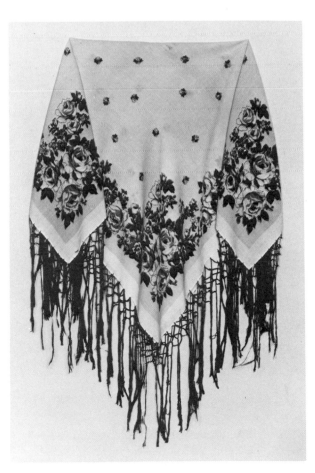

Figure 78. A flowered shawl of lightweight commercial wool—an Italian import—has a heavy fringe added by its Santo Domingo Pueblo owner, about 1964. Length 49" without fringe. (SAR M.552.)

derived category includes the men's cotton pants with outer leg slits and their long, loose commercial cloth shirts, some decorated by drawn work, ribbons, or lace. Red cotton shirts with white openwork overshirts (Fig. 77, Pl. 23) may have been inspired by Catholic church vestments.

Anglo commerce brought Pendleton blankets, gayly patterned shawls (Fig. 78), and squares of commercial cloth that replaced traditional shoulder mantas. The same sorts of brightly colored cloth came to be made into "back aprons," which women wear over their shoulders either alone or under the regular manta (Fig. 79, Pl. 24). Pueblo women also adopted lace-trimmed petticoats and commercial cloth undermantas designed to show at the bottom of the traditional blanket-dress. Other Anglo contributions were aprons with cross-stitch patterns embroidered on them and dresses of several styles that are sometimes worn under the blanket-dress (Fig. 80, page 94). Ribbon shirts, now made by many Pueblo women and sold to Pueblo men, other Indians, and whites, appear to be a pan-Indian style not confined to the Southwest.

A visitor at a Pueblo feast-day dance today can expect to see the dancers costumed principally in traditional, pre-Spanish forms of clothing that are likely, however, to be made from commercial materials. The traditional garments may be combined with some Euro-American items of dress. The chorus is more apt to feature Spanish- and Anglo-derived costumes, with a few pre-Spanish items such as woven belts and hair ties. Far from disappearing, traditional clothing is more in evidence now, and dancers appear in greater numbers, than before World War II. Indeed, the shift from non-Indian articles of clothing back to traditional articles in ceremonies was noted as early as 1930 by Douglas (1930). Pueblo people continue to incorporate commercial materials into their costumes, but in ways that do not destroy the distinctive character of the tradition.

Figure 79. Women wearing commercial cloth back aprons file in front of a
row of Shalako kachinas in a painting by Awa Tsireh (Alfonso Roybal),
about 1934. (SAR P.91.)

Figure 80. This Isleta Pueblo woman has a Euro-American-style cotton dress under her traditional blanket-dress. She also wears a calico apron, a commercial cloth back apron, and a head scarf. (Courtesy Natural History Museum of Los Angeles County, photo by A. C. Vroman.)

Appendix:
The School of American Research Collection of Pueblo Textiles

The School of American Research numbers 135 traditional Pueblo textiles and 62 items of Euro-American style in its collections at the time of this writing (July, 1982). Most were acquired by gift or purchase through the Indian Arts Fund, Inc., from the mid-1920s to 1972, under the direction of the late Drs. Harry P. Mera and Kenneth M. Chapman, and were recorded with the able assistance of Mrs. Betty Toulouse.

The strength of the collection lies in the number and quality of its mid-nineteenth-century pieces. Especially outstanding are the handsome, embroidered black wool mantas from Zuni and Acoma and the two remarkable embroidered white cotton breechcloths from Acoma and Jemez. Because all the categories of traditional textiles are so well represented, it has been possible to characterize them in general terms in the preceding text.

As is the case with collections in most museums, there is very little documentation of the School of American Research pieces, usually no more than the date and manner of acquisition. To determine the approximate date of manufacture and, in a few cases, the Pueblo village where a piece was made, I have used criteria of physical characteristics such as types of yarns and dyes, peculiarities of technique, selvage systems, and certain other clues. I have established these criteria through long study of Pueblo textiles in other museums and private collections and through familiarity with published and unpublished writings on the subject.

It is only within the last ten years or so that extensive analysis of southwestern textile dyes has been undertaken. Recognition of the kind of dye found in a textile enables us to date it with some assurance and opens a door to the consideration of larger questions such as the history of dyes in other parts of the world and the patterns of trade that brought fabrics, yarns, and dyestuffs from eastern North America, England, Spain, and Mexico to southwestern weavers.

I have already referred to Max Saltzman's analysis of dyes on nineteenth-century textiles from Spanish looms in the Rio Grande Valley (Saltzman 1979). His findings are certainly relevant to our understanding of Pueblo and Navajo dyes of the period. Even more important for us in this regard are the analyses currently being carried out by Dr. David Wenger of the University of Colorado Health Science Center under the direction of Dr. Joe Ben Wheat, on red yarns taken from textiles known to be Pueblo or Navajo made. Complete results of their study are not yet published, but yarn samples from eight of the School's pieces—four mantas, two breechcloths, a kilt, and a brocaded sash—have been tested. Six were found to be lac-dyed, and two, cochineal.

Wheat sees lac-dyed yarns in these and other specimens as predominantly very fine, two-ply, loosely s-spun and Z-twisted, and only rarely as z-spun. A museum curator identifying s-Z raveled red yarn would be justified in assuming it to be lac-dyed, thus dating the textile to 1865 or earlier. A word of caution is in order, however. The direction of spin in these fine yarns is not always easy to determine, and in my experience, embroidery yarns in a single piece may vary. In some cases, Wheat and I have not reached agreement on the spin and twist of a yarn.

Cochineal-dyed, raveled and commercial yarns are usually z-spun. Raveled yarns could date from the late 1700s to the 1870s, and three-ply commercial yarns between 1860 and 1875. However, since handspun and commercial synthetic-dyed yarns are also usually z-spun, determining what is and what is not cochineal-dyed is best left to actual testing. The yarn type and dye analysis of embroidery and brocade yarns in the School of American Research collection is summarized in Table 1 (see p. 108).

The following list gives basic information about each Pueblo textile in the School of American Research collection. The pieces are listed by catalogue number within the same categories used in the text. Those pieces illustrated in the text are marked with an asterisk, and, for traditional items, full information about yarns, dyes, and significant technical features is given. Measurements are recorded in inches and centimeters, with the length as measured along the warps always given first for loom-woven pieces. The yarn count, or number of warps and wefts per inch (2.5 cm), is given as (for example) "warps: 10," or "wefts: 15."

Direction of spin, number of plies in a yarn, and direction of final twist in a multiple-ply yarn are recorded as follows:

z or s	single-ply z-spun or s-spun yarn;
Z or S	direction of final twist of a multiple-ply yarn; when used alone, indicates that the number of plies and direction of spin for each ply have not been determined;
z-S	z-spun, S-twist, two-ply yarn; comparable notations are z-Z, s-Z, and s-S;
3z-S	z-spun, S-twist, three-ply yarn; comparable notations are 4z-S, 8s-Z, 3S, and so forth.

In referring to dyes in the following list, "natural" means that the yarn was not dyed, while "vegetal" indicates that a native vegetal dye was presumably used, although the yarns have not been tested. Aniline or other commercial, synthetic dyes are denoted as "synthetic." All reds specified as lac or cochineal have been tested and confirmed by Dr. David Wenger.

Those interested in obtaining more information about the School of American Research collection of Pueblo textiles should write to the Collections Manager, School of American Research, Post Office Box 2188, Santa Fe, New Mexico 87501.

SERAPES AND RUGS

T.1 Zuni, 1870–1880, purchased from Frank C. Applegate, 1925.

T.18 Zuni, 1875–1885, purchased from Clara E. Brentlinger, 1927.

*__T.77__ Zuni, 1870–1880, purchased from E. C. McMechen, 1930. 66" x 45" (168 x 114 cm). Warps: 5; handspun wool, z, natural white. Wefts: 13; handspun wool, z, in natural gray and brown, indigo blue, and synthetic(?) yellow; commercial wool cloth strips, z, in synthetic red. Selvages: warp, pairs of warps knotted, ends form fringes; weft, 2 3z-S indigo blue handspun wool yarns.

*__T.104__ Zuni (?), Moqui pattern, ca. 1860, purchased from Fred Harvey Indian Department, Albuquerque, 1930. 68" x 47" (173 x 119 cm). Warps: 10; handspun wool, z, natural white. Wefts: 49; handspun wool, z, natural white and brown and vegetal indigo blue. Selvages: warp, restored; weft, warps are grouped 3-2-2 from the outer edge in towards the center.

T.186 Zuni, 1870–1880, gift of Dr. A. V. Kidder, 1931.

*__T.309__ Probably Zuni, ca. 1885–1895, gift of Mrs. K. M. Chapman, 1936, originally purchased at Zuni by Col. Frank Grygla, about 1895. 74" x 60" (188 x 152 cm). Warps: 8; handspun wool, z, natural white. Wefts: 20; handspun wool, z, natural white and brown, synthetic gray-blue, red, and orange-yellow. Selvages: original selvages missing.

*__T.323__ Zuni, 1865–1875, purchased from Mabel O'Dell, 1938. 66" x 49" (168 x 124 cm). Warps: 6; handspun wool, z, natural white. Wefts: 27; handspun wool, z, in natural white, black, and gray, indigo blue, and vegetal yellow-green; raveled commercial wool, z, paired, synthetic red. Selvages: restored.

T.336 Zuni, 1875, gift of Andrew Dasburg, 1940.

T.337 Zuni(?), 1870–1880, gift of Andrew Dasburg, 1940.

*__T.347__ 1875–1885, purchased from George C. Travis, 1941. 53" x 43" (135 x 109 cm). Warps: 6; handspun wool, z, natural brown. Wefts: 18; handspun wool, z, in natural white, carded gray, and brown, vegetal(?) yellow, vegetal indigo blue, and synthetic orange, red, and pink. Selvages: restored.

T.379 Zuni or Navajo, 1880s, gift of Mary Cabot Wheelwright, 1942.

*__T.498__ Hopi, 1927, woven by Qoyawayma, Oraibi, purchased from Elizabeth Elder, 1958. 60¼" x 43½" (153 x 110 cm). Warps: 5; handspun wool, z, natural white. Wefts: 16; handspun wool, z, natural white and brown and synthetic purple, orange, and red. Selvages: warp and weft, 2 z-S handspun red wool yarns.

*__T.564__ Hopi, 1930–1950, gift of Margretta S. Dietrich, 1961. 62" x 42½" (157 x 108 cm). Warps: 5; handspun wool, z, natural white and brown. Wefts: 25; handspun wool, z, natural white and brown, vegetal(?) indigo blue, and synthetic red. Selvages: warp and weft, 2 z-S natural brown handspunwool yarns.

T.620 Zuni or Navajo, 1875–1880, gift of Amelia E. White, 1952.

T.626 Probably Zuni, 1880–1900, gift of Amelia E. White, 1952.

*__T.641__ Zuni, Moqui pattern, 1870–1880, gift of Amelia E. White, 1953. 74" x 56" (188 x 142 cm). Warps: 8; handspun wool, z, natural white. Wefts: 34; handspun wool, z, in natural brown and vegetal indigo blue; raveled wool, z, tripled or used in fours, in synthetic orange-red; raveled, crimped wool yarn, s, tripled or used in fours, in synthetic(?) dark red. Selvages: warp, repaired warp ends cut, run back into fabric, 2 4-ply handspun indigo yarns twisted as a regular selvage; weft, no extra selvage yarns, paired warps, 6 pairs on one side and 8 pairs on the other.

HOPI PLAID SHOULDER BLANKETS

*__T.436__ Late 1800s, gift of Amelia E. White, 1945. 24" x 37½" (61 x 95 cm). Warps: 16 brown, 22 white, handspun wool, z, natural. Wefts: 13-15; handspun wool, z, natural white and brown. Selvages: warp, 3 z-S white handspun wool yarns; weft, 2 z-S white handspun wool yarns.

*T.663   1900–1930, gift of Laura Hersloff, 1963, purchased by donor at Hubbell's Trading Post, Arizona, 1930s. 27" x 30" (69 x 76 cm). Warps: 14-15; handspun wool, z, natural tan, indigo blue on natural black, and synthetic purple. Wefts: 14; handspun wool, z, natural white and brown, indigo blue on natural black. Selvages: warp, 3 z-S handspun wool yarns, indigo blue and blue-black; weft, 3 z-S handspun wool yarns, 2 purple, 1 indigo blue.

HOPI WHITE COTTON WEDDING MANTAS

*1981-8-1   1920s or later, gift of Mr. and Mrs. Alden Hayes, 1981. 57" x 81" (145 x 206 cm). Warps: 24; cotton string, 7S, natural white. Wefts: 9; handspun cotton batting, z, natural white. Selvages: warp, 2 cotton string yarns; weft, 2 z-S handspun cotton yarns.

1981-24-1   1920–1940, gift of William Owen Nugent, 1981.

WHITE COTTON MANTAS, EMBROIDERED

*T.11   Zuni, 1926, purchased at Zuni Pueblo by Elizabeth Duggan, 1926. 60" x 72" (152 cm x 183 cm). Warps: 26; commercial cotton string, 3z-S, natural white. Wefts: 13; z, handwoven cotton batting. Embroidery: commercial wool, 4z-S, synthetic black, red, green, orange, and purple. Selvages: warp, 3 z-S handspun white cotton; weft, 2 z-S handspun white cotton.

*T.42   Zuni, 1920s, purchased from C. G. Wallace, 1929. 45" x 59" (114 x 150 cm). Warps: 20; handspun cotton, z, natural white. Wefts: 11; handspun cotton batting, z, natural white. Embroidery: commercial wool, 4z-S, synthetic green, black, orange, and red. Selvages: warp, 3 z-S handspun white cotton; weft, 2 z-S handspun white cotton.

*T.73   1930, purchased from a Santo Domingo Indian, 1930. 43" x 60" (109 x 152 cm). Warps: 30; commercial cotton string, 4z-S, natural white. Wefts: 14; handspun cotton, probably commercial batting, z, natural white. Brocade: commercial wool, 4z-S, synthetic black, green, orange, red, and purple. Selvages: warp and weft, 3 z-S handspun cotton.

T.348   Probably Hopi, 1860–1870, purchased from Ina Sizer Cassidy, 1941. Cut and sewn into a breechcloth.

*T.357   Zuni, 1930s, purchased from H. P. Mera, 1941. 46½" x 38½" (118 x 98 cm). Warps: 14; commercial cotton, 4z-S, natural white. Wefts: border section, 24, commercial cotton thread, paired, 3Z, natural white; center section, 23, commercial wool, 4z-S, natural white. Embroidery: commercial wool, 4z-S, synthetic green, black, orange, yellow, red, and gray-blue. Selvages: warp and weft, 2 white cotton strings, each 2-ply; each ply is a 4z-S string.

*T.404   1925–1935, gift of Rose Dougan, 1943. 44" x 62" (112 x 157 cm). Warps: 22; commercial cotton string, 4z-S, natural white. Wefts: 15; handspun commercial cotton batting, z, natural white. Embroidery: commercial wool, 4z-S, synthetic black, green/blue, red, yellow, and purple. Selvages: warp and weft, 3 z-S handspun white cotton.

WHITE MANTAS WITH RED AND BLUE BORDERS

*T.20   Hopi, 1920s, purchased from Elizabeth Duggan, 1927. 38" x 45" (96 x 114 cm). Warps: 21; commercial cotton string, natural white. Wefts: 18, commercial cotton batting, z, natural white; 48, commercial wool, 4-ply split in two, z, paired, synthetic red; 48, handspun wool, z, synthetic(?) indigo blue. Selvages: warp and weft, 3 z-S yarns.

*T.117   Hopi, 1900–1910, purchased 1930. 29" x 36" (74 x 91 cm). Warps: 33; handspun cotton, z, natural white. Wefts: 22, probably cotton batting, z, natural white; 44, commercial wool, raveled or split from 4-ply yarn, s, single, paired, or tripled, synthetic red; 40, handspun wool, z, vegetal indigo blue. Selvages: warp and weft, 3 z-S handspun indigo blue wool.

T.406   Zuni, 1920s, purchased from Old Santa Fe Trading Post, 1944.

T.427   Pueblo, ca. 1860, anonymous gift, 1944.

T.535   Hopi, 1930–1950, gift of Amelia E. White, 1954.

T.586　1950s, gift of Margretta S. Dietrich, 1961.

BLACK WOOL MANTA-DRESSES

Handwoven

T.23　Hopi, 1850s, purchased from Southwest Arts and Crafts, Santa Fe, 1928.

T.24　Hopi, 1928, purchased from Southwest Arts and Crafts, Santa Fe, 1928.

T.627　1870, gift of Amelia E. White, 1963.

T.692　Santo Domingo, 1870, gift of Mr. and Mrs. Nathaniel A. Owings, 1964.

T.694　Cochiti, 1880s, obtained from Helen Cordero, Cochiti Pueblo, gift of Mr. and Mrs. Nathaniel A. Owings, 1964.

*T.717　Hopi, 1964, woven by Luther Denebe, Old Oraibi, gift of Mr. and Mrs. Nathaniel A. Owings, 1965. 42" x 54" (107 x 137 cm). Warps: 18; handspun wool, z, natural black. Wefts: 18; handspun wool, z, natural(?) brown-black in diagonal twill; commercial wool (probably respun), 4z-S, synthetic blue-black in diamond twill. Selvages: warp and weft, 3 yarns, each consisting of 2 4z-S, commercial blue-black yarns that have been tightly respun and plied together with a Z-twist.

Commercial Cloth

M.544　Santo Domingo, obtained from Helen Coriz, Santo Domingo Pueblo, gift of Mr. and Mrs. Nathaniel A. Owings, 1964.

M.555　Santo Domingo, obtained from Peregrina Reano, Santo Domingo Pueblo, gift of Mr. and Mrs. Nathaniel A. Owings, 1964.

M.618　San Ildefonso, purchased at San Ildefonso Pueblo, 1965.

M.637　Jemez, made by Lucy Lowden, Jemez Pueblo, 1967, gift of Mr. and Mrs. Nathaniel A. Owings, 1967.

ZUNI BLACK WOOL MANTAS WITH EMBROIDERED BORDERS

T.19　1870–1880, purchased from Southwest Arts and Crafts, Santa Fe, 1927.

*T.38　1870–1880, purchased from C. G. Wallace, 1929. 40" x 53" (102 x 135 cm). Warps: 17; handspun wool, z, natural brown. Wefts: 14; handspun wool, z, natural brown. Embroidery: handspun wool, z, vegetal indigo blue. Selvages: warp, whipped with indigo blue yarns, selvage yarns brown, probably 3 z-S yarns; weft, 3 z-S brown yarns, whipped with brown yarns along border section.

T.39　1880, purchased from C. G. Wallace, 1929.

T.45　Mid-1800s, gift of Mary Cabot Wheelwright, 1928.

T.335　Mid-1800s, gift of Andrew Dasburg, 1940.

T.424　Mid-1800s, gift of Mrs. Frank Applegate, 1944.

T.623　1870–1880, gift of Amelia E. White, 1952.

T.624　1880s, gift of Amelia E. White, 1952.

T.625　1870–1880, gift of Amelia E. White, 1952.

T.723　Mid-1800s, purchased from Rex Arrowsmith, Santa Fe, gift of Mr. and Mrs. Nathaniel A. Owings, 1967.

BLACK WOOL MANTAS, EMBROIDERED

*T.44　Possibly Tesuque, 1850–1860, purchased from Nathan B. Stern, 1929. 42" x 59" (107 x 150 cm). Warps: 20; handspun wool, z, black native dye. Wefts: 12; handspun wool, z, black native dye. Embroidery: handspun wool, z, vegetal indigo blue; commercial wool, raveled and respun, z, s, z-Z, and s-S, red lac dye; handspun wool, z, vegetal green. Selvages: warp and weft, 2 z-S handspun black wool yarns.

*T.122　Acoma, 1850–1860, gift of Mary Cabot Wheelwright, 1930. 46" x 55" (117 x 140 cm). Warps: 21; handspun wool, z, natural black. Wefts: 18;

handspun wool, z, natural black in 2/2 twill, vegetal indigo blue in diamond twill. Embroidery: raveled commercial wool, s and z, red lac dye; handspun wool, z, vegetal indigo blue. Selvages: warp and weft, 3 z-S indigo blue handspun wool yarns.

*T.356   San Juan, 1941, purchased from H. P. Mera, 1941. 43½" x 45½" (110 x 116 cm). Warps: 17; handspun wool, z, natural black/brown. Wefts: 18; handspun wool, z, natural black/brown. Embroidery: commercial wool, 4z-S, synthetic red and blue. Selvages: warp, 3(?) z-S handspun black wool yarns, tightly whipped with commercial red thread; weft, 3 z-S handspun dark blue-black yarns, whipped with red at edges of embroidery; the two sets of weft yarns meet at the center of each edge, and selvage yarns are tightly braided to form two 2-inch-long ties at these points.

*T.437   Zuni, 1875–1880, gift of Amelia E. White, 1945. 41" x 57" (104 x 145 cm). Warps: 17; handspun wool, z, natural brown. Wefts: 8; handspun wool, z, black native dye. Embroidery: commercial wool, 3s-Z, 4z-S, and 3z-S, synthetic and natural(?) red. Selvages: warp, 3 heavy z-S handspun brown wool yarns, overcast with red commercial wool yarns of the same type as the 3z-S yarns run in along the weft edges; weft, 3 heavy z-S handspun black wool yarns.

*T.468   Acoma, 1850–1860, purchased from Laura Gilpin, 1948. 48" x 54" (122 x 137 cm). Warps: 18; handspun wool, z, black native dye. Wefts: 15; handspun wool, z, black native dye. Embroidery: raveled commercial wool, z and z-Z, red lac dye; handspun wool, z, vegetal indigo blue. Selvages: warp, 3 z-S handspun brown wool yarns, overcast with fine 3-ply red commercial yarns, with dye that does not appear to be synthetic; weft, 2 z-S handspun brown wool.

*T.699   Acoma(?), originally catalogued Hopi, 1850–1860, gift of Mrs. George Paloheimo, 1964. 48" x 57" (122 x 145 cm). Warps: 16; handspun wool, z, natural(?) brown/black. Wefts: 16; handspun wool, z, natural brown and vegetal black. Embroidery: handspun wool, z, paired, vegetal indigo blue; raveled commercial wool, s-Z paired S, red lac dye. Selvages: warp and weft, 2 z-S brown handspun wool yarns.

MEN'S SHIRTS AND VESTS

Embroidered White Cotton

*T.12   Jemez shirt, 1920, purchased from Frank Toledo, Jemez Pueblo, 1927. Body 46" x 23" (117 x 58 cm), sleeves each 16" wide and 17" long. Commercial cotton sacking. Embroidery: commercial, synthetic-dyed, 4z-S wool yarns.

*T.628   Jemez shirt, ca. 1950, gift of Amelia E. White, 1952. Body 27" x 30" (69 x 76 cm). Heavy, commercial, white cotton cloth; front, back, and sleeves are separate pieces of cloth overcast together with wool yarns. Embroidery: 4z-S commercial wool, red and black.

1978-4-87   Vest, 1940–1950, gift of Harold Gans, 1974.

Indigo Blue Wool

*T.22   Hopi shirt, 1920s, purchased from Southwest Arts and Crafts, Santa Fe, 1928. Body 23 x 21" (118 x 53 cm), sleeves 19½" long, 20" wide at shoulder, 10" wide at cuff. Made from 3 separately woven cloths in 2/2 twill. Warps: 22; handspun wool, z, vegetal indigo blue. Wefts: 15; handspun wool, z, vegetal indigo blue. Selvages: warp and weft, 3 z-S handspun indigo blue wool yarns.

COTTON KILTS

Embroidered

*M.539   Cochiti, 1950–1960, obtained from Paul Trujillo, Cochiti Pueblo, gift of Mr. and Mrs. Nathaniel A. Owings, 1964. 41" x 23¼" (104 x 59 cm). Commercial white cotton cloth. Embroidery: commercial 4z-S yarns in synthetic black, red, and pale green. Black crocheted band sewn to bottom edge, made from commercial 4z-S yarns.

M.553   Santo Domingo, obtained from Peregrina Reano, Santo Domingo Pueblo, 1950–1960, gift of Mr. and Mrs. Nathaniel A. Owings, 1964.

M.554   Santo Domingo, obtained from Peregrina Reano, Santo Domingo Pueblo, 1950–1960, gift of Mr. and Mrs. Nathaniel A. Owings, 1964.

T.169   Hopi, 1920s, gift of Glen G. Skiles, 1930.

T.200   Hopi, 1860–1870, purchased from Fred Harvey Indian Department, Albuquerque, 1932.

T.392   1900, purchased from Ina Sizer Cassidy, 1942.

T.490   1920–1940, gift of Kenneth M. Chapman, 1953.

*T.491   Probably Hopi, 1910–1925, gift of Kenneth M. Chapman, 1953. 47" x 21" (119 x 53 cm). Warps: 28; handspun cotton, z, natural white. Wefts: 11; handspun cotton, z, natural white. Embroidery: commercial wool yarn, 4z-S, synthetic black, red, and green. Selvages: warp (one remains), 3 3z-S handspun cotton yarns; weft (one remains), 2 3z-S handspun cotton yarns. Black wool braid at lower border: 10-strand, ½" wide, made from retwisted commercial yarn.

T.494   1920–1930, purchased from Henrietta Harris, 1953.

T.584   1930–1940, gift of Margretta S. Dietrich, 1961.

T.645   Hopi, 1920–1930, gift of Amelia E. White, 1953.

*T.716   Hopi, gift of Mr. and Mrs. Nathaniel A. Owings, 1965. 57" x 24" (145 x 61 cm). Warps: 21; commercial cotton string, 8z-S, natural white. Wefts: 9; cotton(?), pairs of 1-ply z-spun yarns, possibly handspun, natural white. Embroidery: commercial wool, 4z-S, synthetic black, green, and red. Selvages: warp, 3 z-S handspun cotton yarns; wefts, 2 z-S handspun cotton yarns; selvages are overcast with black wool yarns that are retwisted commercial 4z-S.

1969-42   Santa Ana or Zia, 1920–1930, gift of Amelia E. White, 1969.

1977-5-1   Hopi, 1920–1927, gift of Mr. and Mrs. John Gaw Meem, 1977.

*1978-4-86   Hopi, 1930–1940, gift of Harold Gans, 1974. 43" x 24" (109 x 61 cm). Warps: 23; commercial cotton string, 8z-S, natural white. Wefts: 10; handspun commercial cotton fibers, z, natural white. Embroidery: commercial wool, 4z-S, synthetic black, red, and green. Selvages: warp and weft, 3 commercial cotton strings.

1981-2-13   Cochiti, 1920–1940, gift of Sallie R. Wagner, 1981.

Painted

C.206   Santo Domingo, 1930–1940, anonymous purchase, 1942.

*T.376   1930–1940, purchased from John Bitz, 1942. 40" x 18" (102 x 46 cm). Cotton sacking, painted yellow. Plumed serpents, hands, stars, and crosses painted on in dark green and blue. Along bottom edge is a 2" band of cotton cloth painted green, from which hangs a row of tin tinklers.

EMBROIDERED WHITE COTTON BREECHCLOTHS

*T.93-94   Acoma, 1800–1850, purchased at Acomita by Kenneth M. Chapman, 1930. Two ends of breechcloth, each 16" (41 cm) wide. Warps: 31; handspun cotton, z, natural white. Wefts: 18; handspun cotton, z, natural white. Embroidery: handspun wool, z, vegetal indigo blue, vegetal green, and lac rust. Selvages: warp, 2 z-S handspun white cotton yarns; weft, 2 z-S handspun white cotton yarns overcast with z-S rust wool yarns along outer zone of embroidery. Heavy tassels made by covering a cylinder of corn husks with white cotton yarns and binding them at the lower edge of the cylinder.

*T.395   1800–1850, collected at Jemez Pueblo. 84" x 17" (213 x 43 cm). Warps: 32; handspun cotton, z, natural white. Wefts: 17; handspun, z, natural white. Embroidery: handspun wool, z, vegetal indigo blue; and raveled wool, s-Z, lac red. Selvages: warp, 2 3z-S handspun cotton yarns; weft, 2 z-S handspun cotton yarns. Heavy tassels are of cotton over a hard core.

SASHES WITH ENDS PATTERNED BY "HOPI BROCADE"

T.311 Hopi, 1920–1930, gift of Marion Winnek, 1936.

T.331 Hopi, 1920–1930, gift of Mary Austin, 1939.

T.332 Hopi, 1920s, gift of Mary Austin, 1939.

****T.402** Hopi, 1930s, gift of Rose Dougan, 1943. 90" x 10" (229 x 25 cm). Warps: 26; commercial cotton string, 4z-S, natural white. Wefts: 12; handspun wool, z, natural white. Tabby: 17; commercial cotton string, 3S, natural white. Brocade: 17; commercial wool, 4z-S, synthetic red, turquoise, purple, and black. Selvages: warp, fringe of warp loops at brocaded ends, 2 pairs of red yarns on unfringed ends; weft, 2 pairs of red yarns.

****T.644** Hopi, 1930–1950, gift of Amelia E. White, 1953. 89" x 10¼" (226 x 26 cm). Warps: 16; commercial cotton string, 4z-S, natural white. Wefts: 11; handspun wool, z, natural white. Tabby: 15; commercial cotton string, S, natural white. Brocade: 14; commercial wool, 4z-S, synthetic black, green, purple, and red. Selvages: warp, fringe of warp loops at brocaded ends; unpatterned ends and weft selvages, 2 cords, one red and one green, each of 2 4z-S wool yarns.

T.687 Hopi, 1963, made by Luther Denebe, Old Oraibi, gift of Ernest Von Helms, 1963.

****T.700** Hopi(?), about 1880–1900, gift of Mrs. George A. Paloheimo, 1964. 90" x 10" (228 x 25 cm). Warps: 28; handspun wool, z, natural white. Wefts: 12; handspun wool, z, natural white. Tabby: 17; commercial linen(?) thread , S, natural white. Brocade: 17; handspun wool, z, vegetal indigo blue and pale green; 4z-S, synthetic black and red. Selvages: warp, warp ends twisted together by fours at fringed end, at unfringed ends are 3 pairs of red wool yarns; weft, 2 pairs of red yarns.

****T.712** Hopi, 1860–1875, gift of Mr. and Mrs. Nathaniel A. Owings, 1965. One-half of sash, 10" x 45" (25 x 114 cm). Warps: 22; handspun wool, z, natural white. Wefts: 16; handspun wool, z, natural white. Tabby: 24; commercial linen(?) thread, S, paired, natural white. Brocade: 24 pairs or singles;

commercial wool, Saxony or 3-ply Germantown(?), 3z-S, cochineal red and vegetal(?) tan, brown, and blue-green; handspun wool, z, vegetal indigo blue. Selvages: warp, 3 3-ply red commercial wool yarns twisted through warps above fringe, unfringed end has selvage of 3 3-ply red yarns; weft, 2 3-ply red yarns.

1978-4-84 Hopi, 1930s, gift of Harold Gans, 1974.

1978-4-85 Hopi, 1930s, gift of Harold Gans, 1974.

****1981-2-5** Hopi, 1960, gift of Sallie R. Wagner, 1981. 108" x 12" (274 x 30 cm). Warps: 26; commercial cotton string, 6S, natural white. Wefts: 10; commercial wool, 4z-S, natural white. Tabby: 15, commercial cotton thread, S, natural white. Brocade: 15; commercial wool, 4z-S, synthetic red, green, purple, and black. Selvages: warp, fringe of warp loops at brocaded ends, unfringed ends have 2 green yarns and 2 red yarns respectively; weft, 2 4-ply green commercial wool yarns.

FRINGED WHITE COTTON SASHES

Braided (Sprang)

T.643 1900–1920, gift of Amelia E. White, 1953.

T.657 Late 1800s, gift of Mrs. H. P. Mera, 1962.

T.691 Santo Domingo, 1950–1960, gift of Mr. and Mrs. Nathaniel A. Owings, 1964.

T.695 1960, obtained from Salvador Naranjo, Santa Clara Pueblo, gift of Mr. and Mrs. Nathaniel A. Owings, 1964.

****T.708** Hopi, 1950s, purchased from Peregrina Reano, Santo Domingo Pueblo, who obtained it from a Hopi, gift of Mr. and Mrs. Nathaniel A. Owings, 1964. 92" x 8" (234 x 20 cm). Includes 193 z-S white cotton yarns, probably handspun commercial batting. Corn husk rings, braided and bound with cotton yarns.

1978-1-196 Hopi, 1920–1940(?), gift of Amelia E. White, 1978.

1978-1-197 Hopi, 1950–1960, gift of Amelia E. White, 1978.

Woven

*T.589 Tesuque, 1950s, gift of Margretta S. Dietrich, 1961. 87" x 3" (221 x 8 cm). Plain weave, warps and wefts 4-ply white cotton string, warp-faced with a warp-float pattern. Corn husk rings.

LEGGINGS

Knit

M.529 Santo Domingo, obtained from Maria Coriz, Santo Domingo Pueblo, 1964, gift of Mr. and Mrs. Nathaniel A. Owings, 1964.

*T.497 Hopi, 1945–1955, purchased from Luke Kewanousi at Gallup Intertribal Ceremonial, gift of Margretta S. Dietrich, 1958. 16½" x 4½–5½" (42 x 11–14 cm). Handspun wool, z, natural white. Stockingette stitch with purled top and bottom borders and diamond pattern down one side.

*T.503 San Juan, 1940, gift of Margretta S. Dietrich, 1959. 24" long (61 cm). White commercial 4-ply cotton string. Cable stitch, side fringe.

*1981-2-4 Cochiti, 1975, given to Sallie R. Wagner by Caroline Pecos, Cochiti Pueblo, in 1975, gift of Sallie R. Wagner, 1981. 11" (28 cm) long. Commercial 4-ply black wool yarn. Stockingette stitch with purled band at top and bottom.

Crocheted

*M.647 Isleta, 1972, made by Romalda Lujan, Isleta Pueblo, purchased 1972. 14" (36 cm) long. Shiny white commercial cotton yarn.

BELTS, GARTERS, AND HAIR TIES

Belts

T.85 Navajo style, Zuni, purchased from C. G. Wallace, 1929.

*T.86 Navajo style, Zuni, 1800s(?), purchased from C. G. Wallace, 1929. 108" x 3½" (274 x 9 cm). Warps: (edge) 46, commercial wool, 4z-S, synthetic red; (center) 24 in 3/4", commercial wool, 4z-S, synthetic green, and commercial cotton string, z-S, natural white. Wefts: 11; commercial cotton string, z-S, natural white.

*T.87 Hopi style, Zuni, 1920s, purchased from C. G. Wallace, 1929. 78" x 3½" (198 x 9 cm). Warps: (edge) 32, (center) 44; commercial wool, 4z-S, synthetic red, green, and black. Wefts: 14; commercial cotton thread, z, synthetic black.

T.88 1920s, Hopi style, Zuni, purchased from C. G. Wallace, 1929.

T.89 1920s, Navajo style, purchased from C. G. Wallace, 1929.

T.90 1920s, Navajo style, purchased from C. G. Wallace, 1929.

T.91 1920s, Navajo style, purchased from C. G. Wallace, 1929.

T.92 1920s, Hopi style, purchased from C. G. Wallace, 1929.

*T.98 San Juan, 1920s, purchased from Maria Chavez, San Juan Pueblo, 1929, by Miss A. B. Stoll. 120" x 2 3/4" (305 x 7 cm). Warps: 24; commercial wool, 4z-S, synthetic yellow, tan, rust, and red. Wefts: 8; commercial wool, 4z-S, synthetic yellow.

T.99 1920s, modified Hopi style, San Juan, purchased from Maria Chavez, San Juan Pueblo, by Miss A. B. Stoll, 1929.

T.201 About 1930, Hopi style, Zuni, gift of Tobe Turpen, McAdams Trading Co., 1932.

T.202 About 1930, Hopi style, Zuni, gift of Tobe Turpen, McAdams Trading Co., 1932.

T.391 About 1900, Hopi style, purchased from Ina Sizer Cassidy, 1942.

T.421 Late 1800s, Hopi style, purchased from Bessie S. McKibbin, 1944.

T.501 Hopi style, gift of Trinidad (Mrs. Alfred H.) Herrera, Cochiti Pueblo, 1960.

T.590 Modified Navajo style, gift of Margretta S. Dietrich, 1961.

T.654 About 1960, Navajo or Pueblo, purchased at Hubbell's Trading Post, Arizona, 1961.

T.656 About 1960, Navajo or Pueblo, purchased at Hubbell's Trading Post, Arizona, 1961.

*__T.689__ Hopi style, Santo Domingo, 1960s, obtained from Maria D. Coriz, Santo Domingo Pueblo, gift of Mr. and Mrs. Nathaniel A. Owings, 1964. 112" x 3 3/8" (284 x 9 cm). Warps: (edge) 42, commercial wool, 4z-S, synthetic blue-black; (center) 46, commercial wool, 4z-S, synthetic red and green. Wefts: commercial cotton thread, z, synthetic black.

T.690 About 1960, Hopi style, obtained from Esther Reano, Santo Domingo Pueblo, gift of Mr. and Mrs. Nathaniel A. Owings, 1964.

T.693 About 1960, Hopi style, gift of Mr. and Mrs. Nathaniel A. Owings, 1964.

T.696 About 1960, Hopi style, obtained from Paul Trujillo, Cochiti Pueblo, gift of Mr. and Mrs. Nathaniel A. Owings, 1964.

*__T.701__ Navajo style, Hopi, 1960s, gift of Mrs. George A. Paloheimo, 1964. 106" x 4" (269 x 10 cm). Warps: (edge) 42, commercial wool, 4z-S, synthetic red; (center) 42, commercial wool, 4z-S, synthetic green, and commercial cotton, 4z-S, natural white. Wefts: 12; commercial cotton, 4z-S, natural white.

T.710 About 1960, Hopi style, San Ildefonso, purchased at San Ildefonso, 1965. Gift of Mr. and Mrs. Nathaniel A. Owings, 1965.

*__T.711__ Hopi style, San Ildefonso, 1965, purchased at San Ildefonso, gift of Mr. and Mrs. Nathaniel A. Owings, 1965. 94" x 2½" (239 x 6 cm). Warps: (edge) 32, commercial wool, 4z-S, synthetic red; (center) 12 in ½", commercial wool, 4z-S, synthetic blue. Wefts: 12; commercial cotton, z-S, synthetic black.

*__T.724__ Hopi style, Jemez, made by Lucy Lowden, Jemez Pueblo, 1967, gift of Mr. and Mrs. Nathaniel A. Owings, 1967. 88" x 2½" (224 x 6 cm). Warps: (edge) 32, commercial wool, 4z-S, synthetic red; (center) 33 in

3/4", commercial wool, 4z-S, synthetic green and blue. Wefts: 11; commercial cotton, z-S, synthetic black.

*__1981-20-1__ 1947, purchased at Turpen Trading Post, Gallup, 1947, gift of Jane Snow, 1981. 51" x 2¼" (130 x 6 cm) with fringe. Warps: (edge) 20 in ½", commercial wool, 4z-S, synthetic blue; (center) 47, commercial wool, 4z-S, synthetic black and green. Wefts: 12; commercial wool, s-Z, synthetic black.

Garters

M.648 Isleta, 1972, made by Sofie Salvador, Isleta Pueblo, gift of Mr. and Mrs. Nathaniel A. Owings, 1972.

*__T.41__ Zuni, 1929, purchased from C. G. Wallace, 1929. 36" x 2¼" (91 x 6 cm). Warps: (edge) 22 in ½", commercial wool, 4z-S, synthetic red; (center) 20 in ½", commercial wool, 4z-S, synthetic green and yellow and natural white. Wefts: 9; commercial wool, 4z-S, natural white.

T.591 Gift of Margretta S. Dietrich, 1961.

T.593 Purchased from Ina Sizer Cassidy, 1961.

Hair Tie

*__T.502__ Cochiti, 1960, gift of Trinidad (Mrs. Alfred H.) Herrera, 1960. 35" x 1 1/8" (89 x 3 cm). Warps: 38; commercial wool, 4z-S, synthetic red and blue; commercial cotton, 4z-S, natural white. Wefts 12; commercial cotton, 4z-S, natural white.

EURO-AMERICAN TRADITIONAL ITEMS

Dresses

M.537 Cochiti, obtained from Caroline Pecos, Cochiti Pueblo, gift of Mr. and Mrs. Nathaniel A. Owings, 1964.

M.538 Cochiti, obtained from Caroline Pecos, Cochiti Pueblo, gift of Mr. and Mrs. Nathaniel A. Owings, 1964.

M.541 Cochiti, obtained from Paul Trujillo, Cochiti

Pueblo, worn by Stefanita Herrera, gift of Mr. and Mrs. Nathaniel A. Owings, 1964.

M.556   Santo Domingo, obtained from Peregrina Reano, gift of Mr. and Mrs. Nathaniel A. Owings, 1964.

M.563   San Felipe, gift of Mr. and Mrs. Nathaniel A. Owings, 1964.

M.567   Cochiti, made by Helen Cordero, Cochiti Pueblo, gift of Mr. and Mrs. Nathaniel A. Owings, 1964.

M.568   Cochiti, made by Helen Cordero, Cochiti Pueblo, gift of Mr. and Mrs. Nathaniel A. Owings, 1964.

M.577   Cochiti, gift of Mr. and Mrs. Nathaniel A. Owings, 1964.

M.578   Santo Domingo, gift of Mr. and Mrs. Nathaniel A. Owings, 1964.

M.579   Santa Ana, gift of Mr. and Mrs. Nathaniel A. Owings, 1964.

M.585   Jemez, gift of Mr. and Mrs. Nathaniel A. Owings, 1964.

M.586   Zuni, gift of Mr. and Mrs. Nathaniel A. Owings, 1964.

M.587   Acoma, gift of Mr. and Mrs. Nathaniel A. Owings, 1964.

M.595   Cochiti, gift of Mrs. Thomas E. Curtin, 1964.

M.601   Tesuque, purchased from Lorencita Pino, Tesuque Pueblo, gift of Mr. and Mrs. Nathaniel A. Owings, 1964.

M.605   San Ildefonso, gift of Mr. and Mrs. Nathaniel A. Owings, 1965.

M.610   San Ildefonso, gift of Mr. and Mrs. Nathaniel A. Owings, 1965.

M.636   Jemez, 1967, made by Lucy Lowden, Jemez Pueblo, gift of Mr. and Mrs. Nathaniel A. Owings, 1967.

M.644   Isleta, made by Romalda Lujan, Isleta Pueblo, purchased 1972.

1979-3   San Ildefonso, made by Blue Corn, gift of Mr. and Mrs. Dennis Lyon, 1979.

Mantas

M.557   Santo Domingo, obtained from Peregrina Reano, gift of Mr. and Mrs. Nathaniel A. Owings, 1964.

M.596   Cochiti, gift of Mrs. Thomas E. Curtin, 1964.

M.600   Tesuque, purchased from Lorencita Pino, Tesuque Pueblo, gift of Mr. and Mrs. Nathaniel A. Owings, 1964.

M.602   Tesuque, purchased from Lorencita Pino, Tesuque Pueblo, gift of Mr. and Mrs. Nathaniel A. Owings, 1964.

M.606   San Ildefonso, gift of Mr. and Mrs. Nathaniel A. Owings, 1965.

M.611   San Ildefonso, gift of Mr. and Mrs. Nathaniel A. Owings, 1965.

M.626   San Ildefonso, gift of Mr. and Mrs. Nathaniel A. Owings, 1965.

Shawls and Blankets

M.530   Pendleton shawl, obtained from Maria Coriz, Santo Domingo Pueblo,, gift of Mr. and Mrs. Nathaniel A. Owings, 1964.

M.547   Shawl, obtained from Helen Cordero, Cochiti Pueblo, gift of Mr. and Mrs. Nathaniel A. Owings, 1964.

M.549   Shawl, obtained from Helen Cordero, Cochiti Pueblo, gift of Mr. and Mrs. Nathaniel A. Owings, 1964.

*M.552   Shawl, obtained from Peregrina Reano, Santo Domingo Pueblo, gift of Mr. and Mrs. Nathaniel A. Owings, 1964. 47½" x 49" (121 x 124 cm) without fringe; fringe 14" long. Sheer wool with floral pattern on pink background. Heavy cotton fringe. Tag says "Made in Italy."

M.559   Shawl, obtained from Helen Cordero, Cochiti Pueblo, gift of Mr. and Mrs. Nathaniel A. Owings, 1964.

M.597   Shawl, Cochiti, gift of Mrs. Thomas E. Curtin, 1964.

M.620   "Peyote blanket," Taos, gift of Mr. and Mrs. Nathaniel A. Owings, 1965.

T.706   Man's shoulder blanket, Taos, formerly owned by Tony Luhan, Taos Pueblo, gift of Brice Sewell, 1964.

Aprons

M.535   Obtained from Caroline Pecos, Cochiti Pueblo, gift of Mr. and Mrs. Nathaniel A. Owings, 1964.

M.536   Obtained from Caroline Pecos, Cochiti Pueblo, gift of Mr. and Mrs. Nathaniel A. Owings, 1964.

M.545   Obtained from Maria Coriz, Santo Domingo Pueblo, gift of Mr. and Mrs. Nathaniel A. Owings, 1964.

M.634   Purchased from Anacita Tafoya, Santa Clara Pueblo, 1966.

M.645   Made by Romalda Lujan, Isleta Pueblo, gift of Mr. and Mrs. Nathaniel A. Owings, 1972.

Back Aprons

M.533   Obtained from Caroline Pecos, Cochiti Pueblo, gift of Mr. and Mrs. Nathaniel A. Owings, 1964.

M.534   Obtained from Caroline Pecos, Cochiti Pueblo, gift of Mr. and Mrs. Nathaniel A. Owings, 1964.

M.546   Obtained from Maria Coriz, Santo Domingo Pueblo, gift of Mr. and Mrs. Nathaniel A. Owings, 1964.

M.580   Santa Ana, gift of Mr. and Mrs. Nathaniel A. Owings, 1964.

*M.581   Cochiti, gift of Mr. and Mrs. Nathaniel A. Owings, 1964. 33" x 31½" (84 x 80 cm). White China silk with pattern of colored disks. Red satin ribbon 1½" wide on three sides and extending 4" from the two upper corners.

M.592   Cochiti, gift of Sallie R. Wagner, 1964.

M.602   Obtained from Lorencita Pino, Tesuque Pueblo, gift of Mr. and Mrs. Nathaniel A. Owings, 1964.

M.608   San Ildefonso, gift of Mr. and Mrs. Nathaniel A. Owings, 1965.

M.627   San Ildefonso, gift of Mr. and Mrs. Nathaniel A. Owings, 1964.

*T.500   Cochiti, gift of Mrs. Alfred Herrera, Cochiti Pueblo, 1958. 36" x 37" (91 x 95 cm). White rayon with multicolored floral pattern. Red satin ribbon 1½ inches wide stitched to three edges and extending 13" beyond the two upper corners. Lace edging on red border, 1¼" wide.

Shirts

M.564   Isleta, made by Romalda Lujan, gift of Mr. and Mrs. Nathaniel A. Owings, 1964.

M.582   Cochiti, purchased from Judi Paris, Cochiti Pueblo, gift of Mr. and Mrs. Nathaniel A. Owings, 1964.

M.583   Cochiti, purchased from Judi Paris, Cochiti Pueblo, gift of Mr. and Mrs. Nathaniel A. Owings, 1964.

M.584   Jemez, gift of Mr. and Mrs. Nathaniel A. Owings, 1964.

M.624   San Ildefonso, gift of Mr. and Mrs. Nathaniel A. Owings, 1965.

M.625   San Ildefonso, gift of Mr. and Mrs. Nathaniel A. Owings, 1965.

*M.646   Isleta, made by Romalda Lujan, gift of Mr. and Mrs. Nathaniel A. Owings, 1972. 33" (84 cm) long, sleeves 23½" (59 cm) long. Red cotton shirt with fine-weave white cotton overshirt decorated with lace insets.

*1981-5   Isleta, made by Demacia Lucero Cariz, gift of Paul Masters, 1981. 23" (58 cm) long, sleeves 15" (38 cm) long. Rust-red cotton blouse with white cotton overshirt. Inset at shoulders and down sleeves of overshirt are panels of commercial cotton net with hand-embroidered motifs.

Pants

M.542   Cochiti, obtained from Fred Cordero, Cochiti Pueblo, gift of Mr. and Mrs. Nathaniel A. Owings, 1964.

M.562   Blue jeans, gift of Mrs. Jack Lambert, 1964.

Pants and Shirts

M.566   Drummer's costume, Santo Domingo, gift of Mr. and Mrs. Nathaniel A. Owings, 1964.

M.613   Shirt, San Ildefonso, gift of Mr. and Mrs. Nathaniel A. Owings, 1965.

M.614   Pants, San Ildefonso, gift of Mr. and Mrs. Nathaniel A. Owings, 1965.

Miscellaneous

M.616   Boy's headband, San Ildefonso, gift of Mr. and Mrs. Nathaniel A. Owings, 1965.

TABLE 1

Analysis of red embroidery and brocade yarns in eight Pueblo textiles in the School of American Research collection.

NUMBER	ITEM	PROVENANCE	YARN TYPE	DYE
T.44	Black wool manta, embroidered	Tesuque(?) 1850–1860	Raveled wool, z, z-Z, s, s-S (KPK) s-Z (JBW)	Lac
T.93	Cotton breechcloth, embroidered	Acoma 1800–1850	Handspun wool, z (KPK) Probably raveled and respun, z (JBW)	Lac
T.122	Black wool manta, embroidered	Acoma 1850–1860	Raveled wool, s-Z (JBW) s, paired and Z-twisted between stitches (KPK)	Lac
T.200	Cotton kilt, embroidered	Hopi 1800–1870	Raveled wool, s-S (KPK, JBW)	Cochineal
T.395	Cotton breechcloth, embroidered	Jemez 1800–1850	Raveled wool, s-Z (KPK, JBW)	Lac
T.468	Black wool manta, embroidered	Acoma 1850–1860	Raveled wool, z, z-Z (KPK) s-Z (JBW)	Lac
T.699	Black wool manta, embroidered	Acoma 1850–1860	Raveled wool, s-Z (KPK, JBW)	Lac
T.712	Dance sash, brocaded	Hopi 1860–1875	Commercial, twill-weave wool cloth strip, z (KPK, JBW) Commercial 3-ply Saxony z-S (KPK, JBW)	Cochineal Cochineal

References

BEAGLEHOLE, E.
1937 *Notes on Hopi Economic Life,* Yale University Publications in Anthropology, no.15 (New Haven, Connecticut).

BLOOM, LANSING
1927 "Early Weaving in New Mexico," *New Mexico Historical Review* 2:228–38.

BOHRER, VORSILA L.
In press "The Diffusion and Utilization of Cotton North of Mexico," in *Handbook of North American Indians,* vol. 3 (Washington, D.C.: Smithsonian Institution).

COLLINGWOOD, PETER
1974 *The Techniques of Sprang* (London: Faber and Faber).

COLTON, MARY-RUSSELL F.
1938 *The Arts and Crafts of the Hopi Indians,* Museum Notes, vol. 11, no. 1 (Flagstaff: Museum of Northern Arizona).
1965 *Hopi Dyes,* Bulletin, vol. 41 (Flagstaff: Museum of Northern Arizona).

CRANE, LEO
1913 "Annual Report of the Superintendent of the Moqui Reservation, Keams Canyon, Arizona," *Annual Report of the Commissioner of Indian Affairs* (Washington, D.C.).

DONALDSON, THOMAS
1893 *Moqui Pueblo Indians of Arizona and Pueblo Indians of New Mexico: Extra Census Bulletin* (Washington, D.C.: U.S. Census Printing Office).

DOUGLAS, FREDERIC H.
1930 "Pueblo Indian Clothing," *Indian Leaflet Series,* no. 4 (Denver Art Museum).
1935-38 Unpublished field notes.
1937 "An Embroidered Cotton Garment from Acoma," *Material Culture Notes,* no. 1 (Denver Art Museum).
1938 "Notes on Hopi Brocading," *Plateau* 11:35–38 (Flagstaff: Museum of Northern Arizona).

1939a "Acoma Pueblo Weaving and Embroidery," *Indian Leaflet Series*, no. 89 (Denver Art Museum).

1939b "Weaving in the Tewa Pueblos," *Indian Leaflet Series*, no. 90 (Denver Art Museum).

1939c "Weaving of the Keres Pueblos/Weaving of the Tiwa Pueblos and Jemez," *Indian Leaflet Series*, no. 91, (Denver Art Museum).

1940a "Main Types of Pueblo Woolen Textiles," *Indian Leaflet Series*, no. 92–93 (Denver Art Museum).

1940b "Main Types of Pueblo Woolen Textiles," *Indian Leaflet Series*, no. 94–95 (Denver Art Museum).

1940c "Weaving at Zuni Pueblo," *Indian Leaflet Series*, no. 96–97 (Denver Art Museum).

DUNN, DOROTHY
1968 *American Indian Painting* (Albuquerque: University of New Mexico Press).

DUTTON, BERTHA P.
1963 *Sun Father's Way: The Kiva Murals of Kuaua* (Albuquerque: University of New Mexico Press).

EMERY, IRENE
1966 *The Primary Structures of Fabrics* (Washington, D.C.: The Textile Museum).

FISHER, NORA, AND JOE BEN WHEAT
1979 "The Materials of Southwestern Weaving," in *Spanish Textile Tradition of New Mexico and Colorado*, Museum of International Folk Art (Santa Fe: Museum of New Mexico Press).

FOX, NANCY
1978 *Pueblo Weaving and Textile Arts* (Santa Fe: Museum of New Mexico Press).

GIFFORD, E. W., AND W. EGBERT SCHENCK
1926 *Archaeology of the Southern San Joaquin Valley, California*, University of California Publications in American Archaeology and Ethnology, vol. 23 (Berkeley).

HAMMOND, GEORGE P., AND AGAPITO REY, EDS.
1929 *Expedition into New Mexico Made by Antonio de Espejo, 1582–1583*, Quivira Society Publications, no. 1 (Los Angeles).

HIBBEN, FRANK C.
1975 *Kiva Art of the Anasazi at Pottery Mound* (Las Vegas, Nev.: KC Publications).

HODGE, F. W., GEORGE P. HAMMOND, AND AGAPITO REY
1945 *Fray Alonso de Benavides' Revised Memorial of 1634*, Coronado Cuarto Centennial Publication, 1540–1940, vol. 4 (Albuquerque: University of New Mexico Press).

HOUGH, WALTER
1918 "The Hopi Indian Collection in the United States National Museum," *Proceedings* 54:235–96 (Washington,D.C.: United States National Museum).

JAMES, GEORGE WHARTON
1927 *Indian Blankets and Their Makers* (Chicago: A. C. McClurg and Co.).

JONES, VOLNEY H.
1936 "A Summary of Data on Aboriginal Cotton in the Southwest," in *Symposium on Prehistoric Agriculture,* University of New Mexico, Bulletin, Anthropological Series, vol. 1 (Albuquerque).

KENT, KATE PECK
1940 "The Braiding of a Hopi Wedding Sash," *Plateau* 12:46–52 (Flagstaff: Museum of Northern Arizona).
1957 "The Cultivation and Weaving of Cotton in the Prehistoric Southwestern United States," *Transactions of the American Philosophical Society,* n. s. vol. 47, part 3 (Philadelphia: American Philosophical Society).
1976 "Pueblo and Navajo Weaving Traditions and the Western World," in *Ethnic and Tourist Arts,* ed. by Nelson H. H. Graburn (Berkeley: University of California Press).
1983 *Textiles of the Prehistoric Southwest,* School of American Research Southwest Indian Arts Series (Albuquerque: University of New Mexico Press).
in press "Spanish, Navajo, or Pueblo? A Guide to the Identification of Nineteenth-Century Southwestern Textiles," in *Hispanic Arts and Ethnohistory in the Southwest* (Santa Fe: Spanish Colonial Arts Society).

MACLEISH, KENNETH
1940 "Notes on Hopi Belt-Weaving at Moenkopi," *American Anthropologist* n. s. 42:291–310.

MERA, H. P.
1943 *Pueblo Indian Embroidery,* Laboratory of Anthropology Memoir no. 4 (Santa Fe).

MORRIS, ELIZABETH ANN
1959 *Basketmaker Caves in the Prayer Rock District, Northeastern Arizona,* Anthropological Papers, no. 35 (Tucson: University of Arizona).

MUSEUM OF INTERNATIONAL FOLK ART
1979 *Spanish Textile Tradition of New Mexico and Colorado* (Santa Fe: Museum of New Mexico Press).

NEQUATEWA, EDMUND, AND MARY-RUSSELL F. COLTON
1933 "Hopi Courtship and Marriage", *Museum Notes* 5:41–54 (Flagstaff: Museum of Northern Arizona).

NEVILLE, FREDERICA KARBER
1952 "Clothing Acculturation within Three Indian Tribes," M.S. thesis, Louisiana State University.

NEW MEXICO ASSOCIATION ON INDIAN AFFAIRS
1932 *Annual Report for 1932* (Santa Fe: New Mexico State Records Center and Archives, Box 2).

PALMER, A. D.
1870 "Report of the Commissioner of Indian Affairs," in *Report of the Secretary of the Interior, Messages and Documents, 1870–71,* vol. 1 (Washington, D.C.: Government Printing Office).

PARSONS, ELSIE CLEWS
1939 *Pueblo Indian Religion* (Chicago: University of Chicago Press).

RILEY, CARROLL L.
1975 "The Road to Hawikuh: Trade and Trade Routes to Cibola-Zuni During Late Prehistoric and Early Historic Times," *The Kiva* 41:137–59 (Tucson: Arizona Archaeological and Historical Society).

ROEDIGER, VIRGINIA MORE
1941 *Ceremonial Costumes of the Pueblo Indians* (Berkeley: University of California Press).

SALTZMAN, MAX
1979 "The Dye Analysis," in *Spanish Textile Tradition of New Mexico and Colorado,* Museum of International Folk Art (Santa Fe: Museum of New Mexico Press).

SAYERS, ROBERT
1980 "A Recycled Hopi Manta," *The Kiva* 45:301–15.
1981 "Symbol and Meaning in Hopi Ritual Textile Design," *American Indian Art* 6:70–77.

SCHROEDER, ALBERT H.
1979 "Pueblos Abandoned in Historic Times," in *Handbook of North American Indians,* vol. 9, ed. by Alfonso Ortiz (Washington, D.C.: Smithsonian Institution).

SIMMONS, LEO W., ED.
1942 *Sun Chief, The Autobiography of a Hopi Indian* (New Haven, Conn.: Yale University Press).

SMITH, WATSON
1952 *Kiva Mural Decorations at Awatovi and Kawaika-a,* Papers of the Peabody Museum of Archaeology and Ethnology, vol. 38 (Reports of the Awatovi Expedition, no. 5) (Cambridge, Mass.: Harvard University).

SMITH, WATSON, AND JOHN M. ROBERTS
1954 *Zuni Law, A Field of Values,* Papers of the Peabody Museum of Archaeology and Ethnology, vol. 43, no. 1 (Cambridge, Mass.: Harvard University).

SPICER, EDWARD H.
1962 *Cycles of Conquest* (Tucson: University of Arizona Press).

SPIER, LESLIE
1924 "Zuni Weaving Techniques," *American Anthropologist* 26:64–85.

STEPHEN, ALEXANDER M.
1936 *Hopi Journal,* ed. by Elsie Clews Parsons, Columbia University Contributions to Anthropology, vol. 23, parts 1 and 2 (New York).

STEVENSON, MATILDA COXE
n.d. "Dress and Adornment of the Pueblo Indians," Bureau of American Ethnology manuscript 2093 (Washington, D.C.: National Anthropological Archives, Smithsonian Institution).
1904 *The Zuni Indians: Their Mythology, Esoteric Societies, and Ceremonies,* Annual

Report 23, Bureau of American Ethnology (Washington, D.C.: Smithsonian Institution).

STURTEVANT, WILLIAM C.
1977 "The Hole-and-Slot Heddle," in *Ethnographic Textiles of the Western Hemisphere*, ed. by Irene Emery and Patricia Fiske, Irene Emery Round Table on Museum Textiles (Washington, D.C.: The Textile Museum).

TITIEV, MISCHA
1944 "Old Oraibi, A Study of the Hopi Indians of Third Mesa," *Papers of the Peabody Museum of American Archaeology and Ethnology* 22:1–227 (Cambridge, Mass.: Harvard University).

UDALL, LOUISE
1969 *Me and Mine: The Life Story of Helen Sequaptewa* (Tucson: University of Arizona Press).

UNDERHILL, RUTH M.
1944 *Pueblo Crafts*, Indian Handcraft Series, no. 7 (Phoenix, Ariz.: United States Indian Service, Education Division).

WADE, EDWIN, AND DAVID EVANS
1973 "The Kachina Sash: A Natural Model of the Hopi World," *Western Folklore* 32:1–18.

WEBB, WILLIAM, AND ROBERT A. WEINSTEIN
1973 *Dwellers at the Source: Southwestern Indian Photographs of A. C. Vroman, 1895–1904* (New York: Grossman Publishers).

WHEAT, JOE BEN
1976 "Navajo Textiles," in *Fred Harvey Fine Arts Collection* (Phoenix, Ariz.: The Heard Museum).
1979 "Rio Grande, Pueblo, and Navajo Weavers: Cross-Cultural Influence," in *Spanish Textile Tradition of New Mexico and Colorado*, Museum of International Folk Art (Santa Fe: Museum of New Mexico Press).

WHITING, ALFRED F.
1941 "Report on Hopi Crafts, An Analysis of the Museum of Northern Arizona Hopi Craftsman Show Records, 1930–41," manuscript on file at the Museum of Northern Arizona, Flagstaff.
1969-78 Unpublished notes, letters, and manuscripts in the author's [Kent's] possession.
1975 "A Hopi Rabbitskin Blanket," manuscript on file at the Museum of Northern Arizona.
1977 "Hopi Textiles," in *Ethnographic Textiles of the Western Hemisphere*, ed. by Irene Emery and Patricia Fiske, Irene Emery Round Table on Museum Textiles (Washington, D.C.: The Textile Museum).

WRIGHT, BARTON
1979 *Hopi Material Culture* (Flagstaff: Northland Press and the Heard Museum).

Index

Spanish influence on, 11, 42, 91, *see also* Clothing, ceremonial; *names of individual garments;* ritualized giving of, 13, 41, 55, 56, 61, 81; sixteenth-century, 3, 6; wedding: blankets, 14, 51, 52, mantas, 55–56, robes, 25, sashes, 55, 81; women's: classic period, 12, 62–63, manufactured by Hopis, 13, modern, 15, 16, 63–64, 92, *see also* Clothing, ceremonial; *names of individual garments; see also names of individual garments*
Cochineal, 29, 30, 32, 34, 66
Colors. *See* Dyes; *names of individual garments*
Colton, Mary-Russell F., 24
Contemporary textiles, 24–25
Cord: feather, 89; fur, 89: techniques, 90
Costume. *See* Clothing
Cotton: batting, 19, 30; ceremonial uses of, 26; cultivation of, 5, 16, 26, 27; early use of, 4, 5; Pima, 24; processing of, 26–29: carding, 27, 29, ceremonial, 27–28, ginning, 27–28, spinning, 28–29; symbolic importance of, 26; yarn, handspun, 26, 29; *see also* Cloth: commercial; *names of individual garments*
Crochet, 10, 83. *See also* Shirts: crocheted; Shirts: crochet-trimmed

Dance costumes. *See* Clothing, ceremonial
Decoration. *See* Appliqué; Brocade; Crochet; Drawn work; Embroidery; Hopi: brocade; Lace; Patterns
Denver Art Museum, 66
Designs. *See* Embroidery: motifs; Patterns
Drawn work, 73, 91
Dyes, 31–34: aniline, 12, 32–34; black, 5, 31, 51, 66; brownish-red, 31; chemical testing of, 34; green, 31, 59, 66; indigo, 24, 31, 32, 66:importation of, 11, 31, preparation of, with urine, 31–32, value of, 32; native, 31, 66; natural, 24, 29–34 passim, 59, 66: Anasazi use of, 5, sources of, 31, 32, 34; prehistoric use of, 31; purple, 31; red, 5, 29, 30, 32, 34, 66; synthetic, 30, 34, 59, 64: introduction of, 12, 32; yellow, 5, 31, 59

Embroidery, 38–39: Acoma, 10, 38, 60, 66–71; Anasazi, 38; on borders, 10, 38, 56–60, 65–71, 74; early influences on, 10; fabrics used as basis for, 10, 22, 23, 25, 38, *see also names of individual garments;* Hopi, 55–56, 74; importance of, 10, 23, 39; Jemez, 10, 23; modern, 23, 25, 61; motifs: Acoma, 71, Anasazi, 38, bird, 60, butterfly, 59, 60, 66, diamond-shaped, 59, 66, differences in, among pueblos, 12, 71, floral 10, 65–66, 71, geometric, 66, 71, Hopi, 25, 60, hourglass, 66, on mantas, 59–61, 65–66, negative line, 39, 59, 66, 71, perhistoric, 38, 39, 60, rainbow, 59, 60, rectangle, 74, scalloped, 65, simulating twill weave, 38, sources of, 22, 38, 61, sunflower, 59, symbolism of, 59, 66, 74, 81, terraced triangle, 74, triangle, 59, 66, 74, triangle-and-hook, 60, 74, Zuni, 65–71; Rio Grande Pueblos, 10, 22, 23, 61, 74; Salado, 38; Sinagua, 38; stitches, 38, 39, 65, *see also* Stitches: embroidery; techniques, 39, *see also* Stitches: embroidery; tools, 38, 39; for tourist market, 20, 23, 25, 73; wool, 56; yarns: commercial, 19, 24, 39, 59, handspun, 39, 59, 66, raveled, 29, 39, 59, 60, 66; Zuni, 10, 38, 65–71, 74; *see also names of individual garments; names of individual pueblos*

Feather cord, 4, 89
Feathers, 56
Fibers, 26–31: animal, 4, 82; apocynum (Indian hemp), 4; wild plant, 4; yucca, 4, 90; *see also* Yarns
Finger techniques, 4, 5, 10, 83
Four Corners region, 82
Frijoles Canyon, 83
Fur, 4. *See also* Rabbit-fur blankets
Fur cord, 89, 90

Garters, 13, 86

Hair ties, 13, 86, 92
Havasupai Indians, textile trade, 14
Heddle: hole-and-slot, 11, 38; string-loop, 11, 37, 38, 86
Historical periods of Pueblo textiles, 9–25
Hohokam: kilts, 74; openwork motifs, 60; use of indigo, 31
Hopi: belts, 85, 86; blankets, 13, 49–54; breechcloths, 76; brocade, 12, 22, 24, 76–81: colors of, 78, motifs in, 77, 78, origins of, 76, patterns in, 76, 78, symbolism of, 78–81, techniques of, 76–77; embroidery, 55–56, 74; mantas, 55–56, 61, 62; rabbit-fur blankets, 24, 89–90; rugs, 44, 49; sashes, 81–82; shirts, 71; shoulder blankets, 25, 50–54; socks, 83; textiles: literature on, 7, modern, 23–25
Hopi Craftsman Show, 24–25, 52, 54

Tabby, 76, 77. *See also* Weaves: plain
Taos Pueblo: rabbit-fur blankets, 91; textile trade, 13
Tapestry patterns, 49
Tassels, 24, 56, 65
Techniques. *See* Crochet; Embroidery; Finger
techniques; Fur cord; Knitting; Weaving techniques
Temple, 37,39
Tewas: embroidered mantas, 66; leggings, 85
Textiles: importance of, 41–42; influences on:
Euro-American, 6, 14–19, 23, 91, 92, Spanish, 6,
9–12, 42, 91; prehistoric, 3–6, 90: as antecedents of
modern forms, 51, 55, 61, 82–83, 89; Pueblo,
literature on, 6–7; trade in, 5, 6, 13–14, 55–56, *see
also* Tourist market; *see also* clothing; Weaving
techniques; *names of individual items; names of
individual tribes*
Third Mesa, 25, 52
Ties. *See* Hair ties
Tonto National Monument: embroidery from, 38;
shirts from, 73; textiles from, 51; tie and belt
fragments from, 88
Tools, embroidery, 38, 39
Tools, weaving, 37–38. *See also names of individual
tools*
Tourist market, 7–8, 24, 25: belts for, 85, 88;
brocaded items for, 81; embroidered items for, 20,
23, 25; Pueblo disuse of, 7–8, 19, 25; rugs for, 8,
24; shirts for, 73, 81; vests for, 73, 81
Trade. *See* Textiles: trade in; Tourist market
Traditional fabrics, commercial production of, 21–22
Tribes, Indian. *See names of individual tribes*
Tsegi Canyon, 51
Tularosa Cave, 82–83
Twill. *See* Borders: twill; Weaves: twill

Underdresses, 12, 15, 16, 63, 64, 92
Undergarments, introduction of, 12, 15
University of Colorado Museum, 22
Urine, preparation of indigo with, 31–32

Ventana Cave, 51
Verde Valley, 51
Vests: brocaded, 81; embroidered, 73

Warp: patterns, 53, 85, 86; tension, 34, 38; yarn,
preparation of: for backstap loom, 37–38, for

upright loom, 34; yarns for, 29: cotton string, 16,
24, 30, 77, 82; *see also* Weaving techniques
Warping poles, 34
Warps, numbers of, for types of weaves, 37
Weaves: plain, 37, 51, 53, 54, 55, 61, *see also* Tabby;
prehistoric, *see* Textiles: prehistoric; twill, 37, 53–64
passim: embroidery simulating, 38; *see also* Patterns
Weaving: decline of, 14–25 passim: economic factors
in, 19, 25; techniques, 34–38: belts, 11, 37–38, 86,
88, *see also* Looms: backstrap, Hopi brocade, 76, 77,
mantas, 61–65 passim, prehistoric, 4, 5, 6, 54, 83,
90, rabbit-fur blankets, 90, sashes, 76, 77, 82, 83,
serapes, 43–44, shirts, 71, 73, shoulder blankets,
52–54, *see also* Finger techniques; tools, 37–38
Weft patterns, 5, 53, 60, 71, 73
Wefts: acrylic, 24; cloth-strip, 30; cotton batting, 19,
30; yarns for, 29; *see also* Weaving techniques
White, Amelia E., 20
White House Ruin, 73
Women as embroiderers, 12, 20, 23, 24
Women as weavers, 12, 23, 90
Women's clothing. *See* Clothing: women's
Wool: carding of, 11, 29; introduction of, 11; spinning
of, 11, 29, 30; yarns: commercial, 12, 30, handspun,
19, 26, 29, 64; *see also names of individual garments*

Yarns, 26–31: acrylic, 24; commercial, 12, 19, 24,
30, 39, 59; cotton, 26, 29; cotton-fiber, 30;
embroidery, 19, 24, 29, 39, 59; handspun, 19, 26,
29, 39, 59, 64; multiple-ply, 30; raveled, 11, 14, 39,
59, 60, 66: dyes in, 32, 66, early (bayeta), 29–30,
late (American flannel), 30; single-ply, 29, 30;
S-spun, 29, 30; use of, in dating textiles, 31; wool,
12, 19, 26, 29, 30, 64; Z-spun, 29, 30; *see also*
Fibers
Yellow ocher, 31

Zuni: appliqué, 22, 75; belts, 88; blankets, 44, 49;
breechcloths, 22, 75; embroidery, 10, 38, 65–66;
mantas, 38, 55, 64, 65–66; rugs, 44; shoulder
blankets, 44, 50; socks, 83; textile trade, 3, 5
Zuni Indians: cultivation of cotton, 5; early
twentieth-century weaving, 16; ritual use of cotton,
26